STEP-BY-STEP

50 Classic Rice Recipes

STEP-BY-STEP
50 Classic Rice Recipes

Consultant Editor
Roz Denny

INDEX

First published in 1998 by Lorenz Books

© Anness Publishing Limited 1998

Lorenz Books is an imprint of
Anness Publishing Limited
Hermes House
88–89 Blackfriars Road
London SE1 8HA

This edition published in 1998 for Index

ISBN 1 85967 733 9

A CIP catalogue record for this book is available from the British Library.

Publisher: Joanna Lorenz
Project Editor: Zoe Antoniou
Designer: Joyce Chester
Photographers: Karl Adamson, Edward Allwright, David Armstrong, James Duncan, Michelle Garrett,
Amanda Heywood, Janine Hosegood, David Jordan, William Lingwood, Patrick McLeavey, Michael
Michaels, Thomas Odulate and Juliet Piddington.
Recipes: Kit Chan, Frances Cleary, Roz Denny, Matthew Drennan, Sarah Edmonds, Rafi Fernandez, Silvana
Franco, Shirley Gill, Rosamund Grant, Janine Hosegood, Deh-Ta Hsiung, Shehzad Husain, Peter Jordan,
Manisha Kanani, Soheila Kimberley, Masaki Ko, Ruby Le Bois, Lesley Mackley, Norman MacMillan, Sue
Maggs, Sallie Morris, Elisabeth Lambert Ortiz, Maggie Pannell, Anne Sheasby, Liz Trigg
and Steven Wheeler.
Stylists: Madeleine Brehaut, Elizabeth Wolf Cohen, Clare Hunt, Maria Kelly, Marion McLornan, Blake
Minton and Marion Price.
Food for photography: Jacqueline Clark, Joanne Craig, Katherine Hawkins, Jane Stevenson, Carol Tennant
and Judy Williams.

For all recipes, quantities are given in both metric and imperial measures and, where appropriate,
measures are also given in standard cups and spoons. Follow one set, but not a mixture,
because they are not interchangeable.

Please use medium-sized eggs unless otherwise stated.

Printed and bound in Hong Kong/China

1 3 5 7 9 10 8 6 4 2

Picture on p7 shows (clockwise from top): wild rice, black glutinous rice, Japanese rice, Camargue red
rice, Thai fragrant rice, white glutinous rice and long grain with wild rice (centre).

CONTENTS

INTRODUCTION

Rice is central to many of the world's greatest cuisines and can be used in a host of ways, both savoury and sweet. No other food is quite this versatile. In the West, we have just begun to appreciate the great potential of this glorious grain and instead of relegating it to the side of our plates as an accompaniment, we now look upon rice as the basis of a delicious meal.

Around two-thirds of the world's population are nourished every day on rice. There are thought to be about 7,000 varieties of rice grown across the globe, all with different qualities and characteristics. The term "rice" should be applied to the milled grain only, while the actual plant is known as paddy. Rice is highly recommended by doctors and nutritionists as it is high in carbohydrates and low in fat, making it a healthy form of energy that is also easily digestible.

Rice was one of the first cereals to be cultivated thousands of years ago from a variety of wild grasses in many different parts of Asia. There was no one specific birthplace. The numerous varieties common today in rice-eating countries evolved according to the climate and terrain and the developing agricultural practices of the time. Even today, many new strains of rice continue to be developed.

The main rice-growing regions of the world are China, Japan, India, Indonesia, Thailand, the southern states of the USA and areas of Spain and Italy. The great joy of rice cooking is the incredible variety of dishes one can make. There are the shaped sushi of Japan, the pressed rice cakes of Thailand, pilaus of India, pilaffs of the Middle East, risottos and paellas of the Mediterranean, jambalayas of America and rice 'n' peas of the West Indies – the list can be endless and the variety inspirational.

Types of Rice

Rice is selected for a dish according to the length of the grain. There are two main categories for rice, long and short grain.

Long Grain Rices

Long grain rices (*oryza indica*) contain high levels of amylase starch, which keeps the grains more separate after cooking. They are excellent steamed or baked, in pilaus and salads. Long grain rices are also known collectively as Patna rices because much of the long grain rice sold to Europe originally came from around Patna in India.

Basmati Rice

This long grain rice is highly aromatic and its name means "fragrant" in Hindi. It is ideal for delicate pilaus. Basmati rice benefits from rinsing in a bowl with plenty of cold water and a soaking for 30 minutes before cooking to lighten the grain.

Brown Rice

This long grain rice has its husk removed, leaving a nutritious bran layer. It is therefore higher in fibre and has a slightly nutty taste and chewy texture. This rice can take up to 40 minutes to cook, so more water will be required to allow for this longer cooking time. Brown (and white) long grain rice is available in par-boiled or easy-cook versions, which means that it has been heat treated with high pressure steam, making it non-stick. This does, however, remove much of the natural flavour and the rice can take longer to cook and has an even chewier texture. Brown basmati is lighter than other brown grains and it takes about 25 minutes to cook.

Red Rices

In the wild, rice is actually a light red colour. Sometimes this characteristic is bred back into long grain rices. Examples of these rices are the Wehani rice from California and more recently a semi-wild cultivated red rice from the Camargue, France, similar to buckwheat in flavour.

Thai Rices

Thai fragrant or Thai jasmine are high quality long grain rices that have a slight stickiness to them and a delicate fragrance. They take even less time to cook than basmati and are best cooked by the covered pan/absorption method with one-and-a-quarter-times the volume of water to rice. No salt is added during cooking.

White Rice

This is the most widely used long grain rice and is mild in flavour. Most long grain rice sold in Europe originates from America and is of excellent quality, especially rice that is grown in Arkansas, Texas and California.

Wild Rice

This is not actually a true rice at all but a form of aquatic grass found growing around lakes in Canada and North America. The best type of wild rice is long, dark brown and glossy. The grains should be cooked until they burst open so releasing their natural deliciously nutty aroma. They take up to 50 minutes to cook, and need to be well submerged in water for most of that time. A form of smaller grain, cultivated wild rice is more readily available and cheaper. It can sometimes also be found in a blend with easy-cook long grains.

Short Grain Rices

Short grain rice (*oryza japonica*), or round grain, is high in amylopectin, which gives a starchy quality so that the grains cling together after cooking.

Glutinous Rices

These are more sticky than Thai rices. The name is misleading as the grains contain no gluten. These rices are also ideal for sushi as the rice sticks together for shaping and rolling. Japanese rice is a short grain glutinous rice, easy for picking up and dipping into sauces. Glutinous rices can be black or white and are often used for puddings.

Pudding Rice

Short grain rice is often packaged as pudding rice because the grains absorb much liquid to make a creamy, rich texture that is essential for milk puddings. Short grain rice can be used for risotto, croquettes, sushi and some stir-fried dishes.

Risotto Rices

These short grain rices have high levels of starch. Good risotto rice gives a nice creaminess to a dish yet the grain still retains an *al dente* bite. Some of the best risotto rices are carnaroli, arborio and Vialone Nano. Stock is added gradually when making risotto, but if making paella with this grain, add the stock all at once and simmer without stirring.

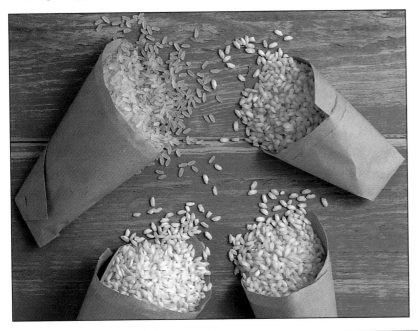

Left (clockwise from top left): arborio and three varieties of carnaroli rices.
Right: brown, long grain, easy-cook, brown basmati, basmati and American long grain rices (centre).

Equipment

The list of equipment that is useful in a kitchen is endless. Some utensils are particularly handy when preparing rice, and will make cooking your favourite dishes so much easier.

Colander
This is essential for draining the water from rice when it has been rinsed or boiled. Use a colander with small holes.

Food Processor
The food processor is useful for mixing and blending ingredients. Most have an attachment for slicing and grating large quantities, which helps to prepare ingredients more quickly, especially since some rice does not take a long time to cook.

Fork
Use a fork to simply fluff up the grains of cooked rice.

Frying Pan
This is useful for sautéed rice. Frying pans are also useful if you are preparing stir-fry recipes when a wok is unavailable.

Hand Whisk
A sturdy hand whisk is useful for beating eggs, combining ingredients such as salad dressings and for mixing sauces to a smooth consistency. The best ones are made of stainless steel.

Measuring Cups and Spoons
Measuring cups and spoons are useful for gauging accurately the volume and corresponding weight of ingredients. Spoon measures range from 2.5 ml/$\frac{1}{2}$ tsp to 15 ml/1 tbsp and cups from 50 ml/2 fl oz/$\frac{1}{4}$ cup to 250 ml/8 fl oz/1 cup.

Mixing Bowls
Glass mixing bowls that fit neatly inside each other are useful for a number of recipe preparations such as making rice salads or mixing desserts.

Pestle and Mortar
This is useful for grinding small amounts of spices, and it is worth buying one if you enjoy cooking with fresh spices regularly.

Rice Cooker
Rice cookers are very useful and make a good investment if you cook rice regularly. They can produce good results with rice, and will free the stove for cooking other ingredients. They are more suitable for cooking sticky and easy-cook grains than basmati rice, which needs to be par-boiled first. A rice cooker will also keep rice warm for up to five hours. Leftover rice can be reheated the following day and the cooker can also be used for steaming many other dishes.

Rice Paddle
This is an ideal utensil for serving cooked rice.

Saucepan
A good stainless-steel saucepan with a tight-fitting lid is essential for cooking rice properly. It is a sound investment for any cook. The best pans tend to be sold individually rather than as a set. They are expensive but will last a lifetime of simmering and boiling.

Steamers
Steamers are used for cooking sticky rice or sticky rice balls. Where these small items are being cooked, line the baskets with pieces of rinsed muslin. Bamboo, stacking-type steamers are available in many sizes from a wide range of stores. When not in use, they look very attractive on a shelf in the kitchen. Like almost all utensils in the oriental kitchen, they are multi-purpose. Indeed the baskets can be used for serving as well as cooking the foods.

Wok
The wok is ideal for stir-frying a number of rice dishes. There are several varieties available including the carbon steel round-bottomed wok or Pau wok. This is best suited to a gas hob, where you will be able to control the amount of heat needed more easily. The carbon steel flat-bottomed wok is best for use on electric or solid fuel hobs, as it will give a better distribution of heat. One useful cooking tip is to warm the wok gently before adding the oil for cooking. The oil then floods easily over the surface of the warm pan and prevents the food from sticking. Less oil is required when using a wok than in conventional pans. Always heat a wok before adding cooking oil.

Right: a selection of some of the most common and useful kitchen utensils.

Plain Long Grain Rice

Use white long grain rice throughout, unless otherwise specified, and remember to adjust your cooking method if using a different grain.

The Open Pan/Fast Boiling Method

This is the simplest method. The rice is cooked in a large amount of boiling water over a medium heat until *al dente*. It is then drained and rinsed. Long grain white rice will take about 15 minutes to cook, and brown rice 30–35 minutes. If using easy-cook rice, follow the directions on the packet.

The Covered Pan/Absorption Method

For this method (shown here) the rice is steamed. The rice simmers gently in a measured amount of water in a covered saucepan until all the water has been absorbed. This has the added bonus of retaining valuable nutrients that would be discarded in the water if the rice were boiled.

Serves 4

INGREDIENTS
250 g/9 oz/1⅓ cups white long grain
 rice
pinch of salt

COOK'S TIP

Precisely how much liquid to use, and the cooking time, will vary depending on the type of rice used, the width of the saucepan (and how snugly its lid fits) and the heat of the hob. For 250 g/9 oz/1⅓ cups brown rice, use 600 ml/1 pint/2½ cups water and cook for 25–35 minutes.

1 Wash the rice in several changes of cold water to remove excess starch, and drain. This is important as the rice is not rinsed at the end, as it is with the boiling method. Place the rice in a saucepan and add 475 ml/16 fl oz/2 cups cold water. (There should be no more than about 1.5 cm/⅔ in of water above the surface of the rice.)

2 Bring to the boil and add the salt, then stir to prevent the rice sticking to the bottom of the pan. Reduce the heat to very, very low, cover the pan tightly and cook for 15–20 minutes, or until all the water has been absorbed.

3 Remove from the heat and leave to stand with the lid on for 5–10 minutes. Fluff up the rice with a fork or spoon just before serving. Rice cooked by the boiling method should also be fluffed up before being served.

VARIATIONS

There are a number of other ways to cook rice. These are more commonly used when rice is cooked with other ingredients in a recipe, such as a stir-fry or bake. Follow the instructions below to sauté or bake rice. See the Covered Pan/Absorption Method (opposite) for quantities and timings but use boiling rather than cold water. You may need more water when cooking by the sauté method.

Rice for Salads

This recipe uses cooked rice. Try to cook rice freshly for a salad rather than use leftover cold rice, as the result is much nicer. This is a basic recipe for a rice salad but you can add a variety of ingredients.

Serves 4

INGREDIENTS
175 g/6 oz/scant 1 cup long grain rice, cooked
75 ml/5 tbsp selected vinaigrette
75 g/3 oz/$^{1}/_{2}$ cup black olives
40 g/1$^{1}/_{2}$ oz/$^{1}/_{2}$ cup chopped spring onions
50 g/2 oz/$^{1}/_{2}$ cup chopped celery
75 g/3 oz/$^{1}/_{2}$ cup chopped radishes
50 g/2 oz/$^{1}/_{2}$ cup chopped cucumber
salt and freshly ground black pepper
parsley sprigs, to garnish

1 Place the cooked, rinsed and drained rice in a bowl and add the vinaigrette of your choice, together with seasoning. Allow the mixture to stand for a good 15 minutes. This method ensures a delicious, light salad where the dressing has been absorbed right into the grain instead of a more cloying dressing that simply coats the side.

2 Quarter the olives, discarding the stones, and add to the rice with the other ingredients. Toss well and garnish with sprigs of parsley.

1 ▲To sauté rice, heat a small amount of oil, butter, or a mixture of the two in a saucepan over a medium heat. Add the rice and stir to coat the grains. Sauté for 2–3 minutes, stirring constantly.

2 Add the measured quantity of boiling salted water. Bring back to the boil, then cover and steam over a very low heat until all the water has been absorbed and the rice is tender.

1 ▲To bake rice, preheat the oven to 180°C/350°F/Gas 4. Place the washed and rinsed rice in a baking dish and add the measured boiling salted water.

2 Cover tightly with foil or a lid and bake until the water has been absorbed and the rice is tender; 20–30 minutes for white rice and 35–40 for brown. Cooking time depends on many factors, including how tightly covered the dish is.

REHEATING RICE

Always reheat cooked rice thoroughly for at least 5 minutes until it is piping hot, especially if stir-frying. This is very important, as cooked rice can harbour spores of bacteria. If rice is reheated on several occasions, or kept warm for a long time, the bacteria may germinate and multiply. Food poisoning could result.

STORING RICE

Cooked leftover rice can be stored for up to 2 days in the fridge. Rice can be frozen, but this affects the starch granules, making them seem chalky when reheated.

Basmati Rice

In India, basmati rice is consumed in great quantities by all members of society. Using ghee instead of butter or oil creates an authentic flavour.

Serves 4

INGREDIENTS
4 ml/³/₄ tsp ghee, unsalted butter or olive oil
250 g/9 oz/1¹/₃ cups basmati rice, washed and drained
salt, to taste

1 Heat the ghee, butter or oil in a saucepan and sauté the drained rice thoroughly for about 2–3 minutes.

2 Add 475 ml/16 fl oz/2 cups of water and salt and bring to the boil. Reduce the heat to low, cover and cook gently for 15–20 minutes until all the water is absorbed. Stand, covered, for 5 minutes. Fluff the grains before serving.

Jasmine Rice

A naturally aromatic, long grain white rice, jasmine rice is the staple of most Thai meals. Salt is not added to this delicate rice during cooking.

Serves 4

INGREDIENTS
350 g/12 oz/1³/₄ cups jasmine rice

1 Rinse the rice thoroughly in cold water, until the water runs clear. Place the rice in a heavy-based saucepan and add 600 ml/1 pint/2¹/₂ cups cold water. Bring the rice to a vigorous boil, uncovered, over a high heat.

2 Stir and reduce the heat to low. Cover and simmer for 12–15 minutes, or until all the water has been absorbed. Remove from the heat and leave to stand for 10 minutes. Fluff up and separate the grains with a fork.

Wild Rice

This aquatic grass is deliciously nutty and firm. It is cooked in the same way as long grain rice, but needs a longer cooking time.

Serves 4

INGREDIENTS
pinch of salt
250 g/9 oz/generous 1 cup wild rice

1 Place 1 litre/1³/₄ pints/4 cups cold water in a saucepan and add the salt. Bring to the boil.

2 ▲ Add the rice to the saucepan and bring back to the boil. Cook the rice for about 45–50 minutes. The rice is ready when it has become tender but still firm and the grains have begun to split open. Drain well and serve.

COOK'S TIP
Wild rice perfectly complements meat and poultry dishes. It is also an excellent partner for vegetables such as winter squashes and mushrooms.

Glutinous Rice

The term glutinous is a little misleading as the rice does not actually contain gluten. It is also known as sticky rice and can be black as well as white.

Serves 4

INGREDIENTS
450 g/1 lb/2²/₃ cups glutinous (sticky) rice
5 ml/1 tsp vegetable oil
2.5 ml/¹/₂ tsp salt

1 Rinse the rice in cold water until it runs clear. Place in a bowl with plenty of water and leave to soak for 1 hour.

2 ▲ Drain, tip into a bowl and add the oil and salt. Line a large steamer with a piece of clean muslin or cheesecloth. Transfer the rice to this. Steam over boiling water for about 45 minutes, stirring from time to time.

COOK'S TIP
Glutinous rice is often served as a pudding, particularly in Thailand. It can be accompanied simply with sugar and coconut cream.

Risotto Rice

This short grain rice absorbs cooking liquid and becomes beautifully creamy. A risotto can be served as a first course, a main dish or an accompaniment. This recipe is basic but flavoursome. The garlic can be omitted.

Serves 4

INGREDIENTS
1.3 litres/2¼ pints/5½ cups chicken stock
25 g/1 oz/2 tbsp butter or oil
½ onion, chopped
2 garlic cloves, crushed (optional)
350 g/12 oz/1¾ cups risotto rice

oil

onion

garlic

risotto rice

chicken stock

1 In a saucepan, bring the stock to the boil, then reduce the heat so that the liquid is kept at a gentle simmer.

2 Heat the butter or oil, or a mixture of the two, in a wide, heavy saucepan. Add the chopped onion and crushed garlic, if using, and cook over a low heat until soft, stirring occasionally.

COOK'S TIP

You can use arborio rice for risottos throughout, if you like, as it is a good medium grain risotto rice, while superfine arborio rice is one of the best. This swells to at least three times its original size during cooking, which enables the rice to absorb all the cooking liquid for a creamy, smooth texture while still retaining the shape of the grains.

3 Add the rice and stir to coat it with the fat. Sauté for 1–2 minutes over a moderate heat, stirring.

4 Add a little of the simmering stock (about a ladleful) and stir well. Simmer, stirring frequently, until the rice has absorbed almost all the liquid.

5 Add a little more of the simmering stock and cook, stirring, until it is almost all absorbed. Continue adding the stock in this way until the grains of rice are tender but still firm to the bite, or *al dente*, and the risotto is creamy but not runny. You may not need to add all the stock. Total cooking time will be about 30 minutes.

Japanese Rice for Sushi

The Japanese prefer their rice slightly sticky so that it can be easily eaten with chopsticks, shaped into rice balls or used to make sushi. Use Japanese rice if you can find it, otherwise substitute Thai or long grain rice.

Serves 4

INGREDIENTS
350 g/12 oz/1³/₄ cups Japanese rice, washed and drained
1 piece giant kelp, 5 cm/2 in square (optional)

MIXED VINEGAR
45 ml/3 tbsp rice vinegar or distilled white vinegar
45 ml/3 tbsp granulated sugar
10 ml/2 tsp sea salt

kelp

Japanese rice

salt

sugar

rice vinegar

1 Place the rice in a large heavy saucepan, cover with 1.2 litres/2 pints/ 5 cups boiling water and add the kelp, if using. Stir once and simmer, uncovered, for 15 minutes. Turn off the heat, cover and stand for a further 5 minutes to allow the rice to finish cooking in its own steam. Before serving, the rice should be fluffed with chopsticks or a fork. This rice is a Japanese staple.

COOK'S TIP

The washing process for Japanese rice is very important as it improves the flavour of the cooked rice. It must be washed several times in cold water until the water runs clear. Thai or long grain rice should only be washed once for sushi recipes, so that the grains become slightly sticky when cooked. Note that cooked Japanese rice should not be stored in the fridge as it will go hard.

2 To prepare sushi rice, make the dressing by heating the vinegar in a small saucepan, with a lid to keep in the strong vapours. Add the sugar and salt and dissolve. Allow to cool. Spread the cooked rice on to a mat or tray and allow to cool.

3 Pour on the dressing and fluff with chopsticks or a fork. Keep covered until ready to use.

Beef and Rice Soup

This classic Iranian soup, *Aashe Maste*, is extremely substantial and almost makes a meal in itself. It is full of invigorating herbs, and is a popular cold weather dish.

Serves 6

INGREDIENTS

2 large onions
30 ml/2 tbsp oil
15 ml/1 tbsp ground turmeric
90 g/3½ oz/½ cup yellow split peas
225 g/8 oz minced beef
200 g/7 oz/1 cup long grain rice
45 ml/3 tbsp each chopped fresh parsley, coriander and chives
2-3 saffron strands
15 g/½ oz/1 tbsp butter
1 large garlic clove, finely chopped
60 ml/4 tbsp chopped fresh mint
salt and freshly ground black pepper
yogurt and naan bread, to serve

onions   *oil*

yellow split peas   *minced beef*   *garlic*

ground turmeric   *saffron*

parsley

chives

long grain rice   *yogurt*

mint   *coriander*   *butter*

1 Chop one of the onions then heat the oil in a large saucepan and fry the onion until golden brown. Add the turmeric, split peas and 1.2 litres/2 pints/ 5 cups water, bring to the boil, then reduce the heat and simmer for about 20 minutes.

2 Grate the other onion into a bowl, add the minced beef and seasoning and mix well. Using your hands, form the mixture into small balls, about the size of walnuts. Carefully add to the pan and simmer for 10 minutes.

3 Add the rice, then stir in the parsley, coriander, and chives and simmer for about 30 minutes, until the rice is tender, stirring frequently. Infuse the saffron in 15 ml/1 tbsp boiling water.

4 Melt the butter in a small pan and gently fry the garlic. Add the mint, stir briefly and sprinkle over the soup with the saffron and its liquid. Spoon the soup into warmed serving dishes and serve with yogurt and naan bread.

COOK'S TIP

Fresh spinach is also delicious in this soup. Add 50 g/2 oz finely chopped spinach leaves to the soup with the parsley, coriander and chives.

Stuffed Vine Leaves

Based on the Greek dolmades, but with a vegetarian brown rice stuffing, this makes an excellent starter, snack or buffet dish.

Makes about 40

INGREDIENTS

15 ml/1 tbsp sunflower oil
5 ml/1 tsp sesame oil
1 onion, finely chopped
225 g/8 oz/1¼ cups brown rice
600 ml/1 pint/2½ cups vegetable
  stock
1 small yellow pepper, seeded and
  finely chopped
115 g/4 oz/½ cup ready-to-eat dried
  apricots, finely chopped
2 lemons
50 g/2 oz/⅔ cup pine nuts
45 ml/3 tbsp chopped fresh parsley
30 ml/2 tbsp chopped fresh mint
2.5 ml/½ tsp mixed spice
225 g/8 oz packet vine leaves
  preserved in brine, drained
30 ml/2 tbsp olive oil
freshly ground black pepper
lemon wedges, to garnish

TO SERVE

300 ml/½ pint/1¼ cups low-fat
  natural yogurt
30 ml/2 tbsp chopped mixed fresh
  herbs
cayenne pepper

yogurt *cayenne pepper*

mint *mixed herbs*

pine nuts

onion

sunflower oil *sesame oil* *yellow pepper* *parsley* *olive oil* *vine leaves*

mixed spice

brown rice *vegetable stock* *dried apricots* *lemons*

1 Heat the sunflower and sesame oils together in a large saucepan. Add the onion and cook gently for 5 minutes to soften. Add the rice, stirring to coat the grains in oil. Pour in the stock, bring to the boil, then lower the heat, cover the pan and simmer for 30 minutes, or until the rice is tender but *al dente*.

2 Stir in the chopped pepper and apricots, with a little more stock if necessary. Replace the lid and cook for a further 5 minutes. Grate the rind from one of the lemons then squeeze both.

4 Bring a saucepan of water to the boil and blanch the vine leaves for 5 minutes. Drain the leaves well, then lay them shiny side down on a board. Cut out any coarse stalks. Place a heap of the rice mixture in the centre of each vine leaf. Fold the stem end over, then the sides and pointed end to make neat parcels.

3 Drain off any stock which has not been absorbed by the rice. Stir in the pine nuts, herbs, mixed spice, grated lemon rind and half the juice. Season with pepper and set aside.

5 Pack the parcels closely together in a shallow serving dish. Mix the remaining lemon juice with the olive oil. Pour the mixture over the vine leaves, cover and chill before serving. Garnish with lemon wedges. Spoon the yogurt into a bowl, stir in the chopped herbs and sprinkle with a little cayenne. Serve with the stuffed vine leaves.

COOK'S TIP

If vine leaves are not available, the leaves of Swiss chard, young spinach or cabbage can be used instead.

Thai Rice Cakes with Spicy Dipping Sauce

Start cooking this recipe the day before you want to serve it, as it involves some lengthy preparation.

Serves 4-6

INGREDIENTS
175 g/6 oz/scant 1 cup jasmine rice
oil for deep-fat frying and greasing

FOR THE SPICY DIPPING SAUCE
6-8 dried chillies
2.5 ml/¹⁄₂ tsp salt
2 shallots, chopped
2 garlic cloves, chopped
4 coriander roots
10 white peppercorns
250 ml/8 fl oz/1 cup coconut milk
5 ml/1 tsp shrimp paste
115 g/4 oz minced pork
115 g/4 oz cherry tomatoes, chopped
15 ml/1 tbsp fish sauce
15 ml/1 tbsp palm sugar
30 ml/2 tbsp tamarind juice
30 ml/2 tbsp coarsely chopped
    roasted peanuts
2 spring onions, finely chopped
mint sprigs, to garnish

oil
dried chillies
shallots
shrimp paste
cherry tomatoes
spring onions
roasted peanuts
jasmine rice
garlic
coriander roots
coconut milk
white peppercorns
minced pork
fish sauce
tamarind juice

1 Make the sauce. Cut along the stem of each chilli and remove most of the seeds. Soak the chillies in warm water for 20 minutes. Drain and transfer to a mortar. Add the salt and grind with a pestle until crushed. Add the shallots, garlic, coriander roots and peppercorns. Pound to make a coarse paste.

2 Pour the coconut milk into a saucepan and boil until it begins to separate. Add the chilli paste. Cook for 2–3 minutes, stir in the shrimp paste and cook for 1 minute. Add the pork and cook for 5–10 minutes, stirring well.

3 Add the tomatoes, fish sauce, palm sugar and tamarind juice. Simmer until the sauce thickens. Stir in the chopped peanuts and spring onions. Remove from the heat and leave to cool. Chill the mixture overnight.

4 Wash the rice. Place in a saucepan, add 300 ml/¹⁄₂ pint/1¹⁄₄ cups water and cover. Bring to the boil, reduce the heat and simmer for 12–15 minutes. Remove the lid and fluff up the rice. Turn out on to a lightly greased tray and press down. Leave to dry out overnight in a very low oven until dry and firm.

5 Remove the rice from the tray and break into bite-size pieces. Heat the oil in a wok or deep-fat fryer. Deep fry the rice cakes in batches for about 1 minute, until they puff up, taking care not to brown them too much. Remove and drain. Garnish with mint sprigs and serve with the spicy dipping sauce.

Sticky Rice Balls Filled with Chicken

These balls can either be steamed or deep fried. The fried versions are crunchy and are excellent for serving at drinks parties.

Makes about 30

INGREDIENTS
450 g/1 lb minced chicken
1 egg
15 ml/1 tbsp tapioca flour
4 spring onions, finely chopped
30 ml/2 tbsp chopped fresh
   coriander
30 ml/2 tbsp fish sauce
pinch of sugar
75 g/3 oz/⅓ cup glutinous (sticky)
   rice, cooked
banana leaves
oil for brushing
freshly ground black pepper
sweet chilli sauce, to serve

FOR THE GARNISH
1 small carrot, shredded
1 red pepper, cut into strips
snipped chives

spring onions · *glutinous rice* · *tapioca flour* · *oil*

minced chicken · *egg* · *sugar* · *coriander* · *banana leaves*

fish sauce · *carrot*

chives · *sweet chilli sauce* · *red pepper*

1 In a mixing bowl, combine the minced chicken, egg, tapioca flour, spring onions and coriander. Mix well and season with fish sauce, sugar and freshly ground black pepper.

COOK'S TIP
Try to find banana leaves for this recipe as they impart their own subtle flavour of fine tea. The leaves are used in Thai cooking for wrapping foods as well as lining steamers.

2 Using chopsticks, spread the cooked sticky rice on a plate or flat tray.

3 Place teaspoonfuls of some of the chicken mixture on the bed of rice, placing them evenly spaced apart. With damp hands, roll and shape this mixture in the rice to make a ball about the size of a walnut. Repeat with the rest of the chicken mixture.

4 Line a bamboo steamer with banana leaves and lightly brush them with oil. Place the chicken balls on the leaves, spacing well apart to prevent them from sticking together. Steam over a high heat for about 10 minutes or until cooked. Remove and arrange on serving plates. Garnish with shredded carrot, red pepper and chives. Serve with sweet chilli sauce as a dip.

Rice Balls Filled with Manchego Cheese

For a really impressive Spanish tapa-style snack, serve these delicious rice balls.

Serves 6

INGREDIENTS
1 globe artichoke
50 g/2 oz/¼ cup butter
1 small onion, finely chopped
1 garlic clove, finely chopped
115 g/4 oz/⅔ cup risotto rice
450 ml/¾ pint/scant 2 cups hot
    chicken stock
50 g/2 oz/⅔ cup freshly grated
    Parmesan cheese
150 g/5 oz Manchego cheese, very
    finely diced
45–60 ml/3–4 tbsp polenta
olive oil for frying
salt and freshly ground black pepper
flat leaf parsley, to garnish

artichoke   onion   butter

polenta   risotto rice

chicken stock   garlic   Parmesan cheese

olive oil   Manchego cheese   flat leaf parsley

1 Remove the stalk, leaves and choke to leave just the heart of the artichoke. Chop the heart finely.

2 Melt the butter in a saucepan and gently fry the chopped artichoke heart, onion and garlic for 5 minutes until softened. Stir in the rice and cook for about 1 minute.

COOK'S TIP
Manchego cheese is made with sheep's milk from La Mancha in Spain. It is ideal for grating or grilling.

3 Keeping the heat fairly high, gradually add the stock, stirring constantly until all the liquid has been absorbed and the rice is cooked – this should take about 20 minutes. Season well, then stir in the Parmesan. Transfer to a bowl. Leave to cool, then cover and chill for at least 2 hours.

4 Spoon about 15 ml/1 tbsp of the mixture into one hand, flatten slightly, and place a few pieces of diced Manchego cheese in the centre. Shape to make a small ball. Flatten, then lightly roll in the polenta. Make about 12 cakes in total. Shallow fry in hot olive oil for about 4–5 minutes until the rice cakes are crisp and golden brown. Drain on kitchen paper and serve hot, garnished with parsley.

Rice Omelette

Rice is an unusual omelette filling in the West, but Japanese children love this recipe, and often top the omelettes with tomato ketchup.

Serves 4

INGREDIENTS

115 g/4 oz skinless, boneless chicken thighs, cut into 1 cm/½ in cubes
35 ml/7 tsp butter
1 small onion, chopped
1 carrot, chopped
2 shiitake or closed cup mushrooms, stems removed, caps chopped
15 ml/1 tbsp finely chopped fresh parsley
150 g/5 oz/¾ cup Japanese rice, cooked
30 ml/2 tbsp tomato ketchup
6 large eggs
60 ml/4 tbsp milk
salt and freshly ground black or white pepper
fresh parsley sprigs, to garnish
tomato ketchup, to serve (optional)

chicken thighs

butter

onion

carrot

mushrooms

milk

Japanese rice

tomato ketchup

parsley

eggs

1 Season the chicken with salt and pepper. Melt 7.5 ml/1½ tsp butter in a frying pan. Fry the onion for 1 minute, then add the chicken and fry until the chicken is white and cooked. Add the carrots and mushrooms, stir-fry until soft over a moderate heat, then add the parsley. Set this mixture aside and wipe the frying pan clean.

2 Melt 7.5 ml/1½ tsp butter in the frying pan, add the rice and stir well. Mix in the fried ingredients, tomato ketchup and pepper. Stir well, adding salt to taste if necessary. Keep the mixture warm. Beat the eggs lightly, add the milk, 2.5 ml/½ tsp salt and pepper.

COOK'S TIP

Shiitake mushrooms are the most popular ones in Japan. They have a good flavour, especially when dried. If they are dried, soak them in a bowl of cold water for 20 minutes, placing a small saucer on top to keep the mushrooms submerged. Drain, but keep the soaking water if you like, as it makes a good stock.

3 Melt 5 ml/1 tsp butter in an omelette pan over a moderate heat. Pour in a quarter of the egg mixture and stir it briefly with a fork, then leave to set for 1 minute. Top with a quarter of the rice mixture.

4 Fold the omelette over the rice and slide it to the edge of the pan to shape it into a curve. Do not cook the omelette too much. Invert the omelette on to a warmed plate, cover with kitchen paper and press neatly into a rectangular shape. Cook another three omelettes from the remaining ingredients. Serve immediately with tomato ketchup drizzled on top, if you like. Garnish with parsley.

Rice Croquettes

These delicious croquettes are actually made from paella and are served as a tapa, a snack or a starter, in Spain. The paella is cooked from scratch here, but you can use leftover paella instead.

Serves 4

INGREDIENTS
pinch of saffron strands
150 ml/¼ pint/⅔ cup white wine
30 ml/2 tbsp olive oil
1 small onion, finely chopped
1 garlic clove, finely chopped
115 g/4 oz/⅔ cup risotto rice
300 ml/½ pint/1¼ cups hot chicken stock
50 g/2 oz cooked prawns, peeled, deveined and roughly chopped
50 g/2 oz cooked chicken, roughly chopped
50 g/2 oz/½ cup petits pois, thawed if frozen
30 ml/2 tbsp freshly grated Parmesan cheese
1 egg, beaten
30 ml/2 tbsp milk
75 g/3 oz/1½ cups fresh white breadcrumbs
vegetable or olive oil, for frying
salt and freshly ground black pepper
fresh flat leaf parsley, to garnish

saffron

white wine

olive oil

risotto rice

chicken stock

egg

parsley

oil

garlic

onion

Parmesan cheese

prawns

cooked chicken

petits pois

milk

breadcrumbs

1 Stir the saffron into the wine in a small bowl and set aside. Heat the oil in a heavy-based saucepan and gently fry the onion and garlic for 5 minutes until softened. Stir in the rice and cook for another minute.

2 Keeping the heat fairly high, add the wine and saffron mixture to the pan, stirring until it has all been absorbed. Gradually add the stock, stirring until all the liquid has been absorbed and the rice is cooked – this should take about 20 minutes.

3 Stir in the prawns, chicken, petits pois and freshly grated Parmesan and stir well, cooking for 2–3 minutes. Season to taste with salt and pepper. Allow to cool slightly, then use two tablespoons to shape the mixture into 16 small croquettes.

4 Mix the egg and milk in a shallow bowl. Spread out the breadcrumbs on a large flat plate. Dip the croquettes in the egg mixture, then roll them in the breadcrumbs to coat them. Heat the oil in a large frying pan. Shallow fry the croquettes for 4–5 minutes until crisp and golden brown. Drain on kitchen paper and serve hot, garnished with a sprig of flat leaf parsley.

Sushi

This recipe shows one of the simplest forms of rolled sushi. You will need a bamboo mat (*makisu*) for the rolling process.

Makes 12 rolls or 72 slices

INGREDIENTS
6 sheets yaki-nori seaweed

FOR THE FILLING
200 g/7 oz block raw tuna
200 g/7 oz block raw salmon
$\frac{1}{2}$ cucumber, quartered lengthways
    and seeds removed
wasabi paste (green horseradish)
gari (ginger pickles), to garnish
Japanese soy sauce, to serve

FOR THE SUSHI RICE
45 ml/3 tbsp rice vinegar
45 ml/3 tbsp granulated sugar
10 ml/2 tsp sea salt
350 g/12 oz/1¾ cups Japanese rice,
    cooked

yaki-nori seaweed

tuna

sea salt

salmon

cucumber

wasabi paste

rice vinegar

soy sauce *Japanese rice* *sugar*

1 To prepare the sushi rice, first make a dressing by heating the vinegar in a small saucepan, with a lid to keep in the strong vapours. Add the sugar and salt and dissolve. Allow to cool. Spread the cooked rice on to a mat or tray. Pour on the dressing and fluff with chopsticks or a fork. Leave aside to cool.

COOK'S TIP

Japanese ingredients can be found in specialist food shops. When you buy the raw fish, make sure that it is for *sashimi*, or for use as raw fish, which means it must be particularly clean and fresh. You may be unaccustomed to using some of the ingredients included in this recipe. Take care when using wasabi paste as it is extremely hot. It is also worth noting that Japanese soy sauce is different to the Chinese version, so do try to locate this for the recipe.

2 Cut the nori in half lengthways. Place a sheet of nori, shiny side downwards, on a bamboo mat on a chopping board. Divide the cooked rice in half in its bowl, then mark each half into six, making 12 portions in all. Spread one portion of rice over the nori with your fingers, leaving a 1 cm/½ in space uncovered at the top and bottom of the nori.

4 Holding the mat and the edge of the nori nearest to you, roll up the nori and rice tightly into a tube with the tuna in the middle. Use the mat as a guide – do not roll it into the food.

3 Cut the tuna, the salmon and the cucumber into four long sticks each. The sticks should be the same length as the long side of the nori and the ends should measure 1 cm/½ in square, Spread a little wasabi paste in a horizontal line along the middle of the rice and lay a stick of tuna on this.

5 Carefully roll the sushi off the mat. Make 11 more rolls in the same way, four filled with salmon, four with tuna and four with cucumber. Do not use wasabi with the cucumber as the paste will make it discolour and soften. Use a wet knife to cut each roll into six slices and stand these on a platter. Wipe and rinse the knife occasionally between cuts. Garnish the sushi with gari, to refresh the palate between bites, and serve with soy sauce.

Paella

Based on the classic Spanish recipe, seafood and bacon are cooked with aromatic saffron rice.

Serves 6

INGREDIENTS

30 ml/2 tbsp olive oil

2 red peppers, seeded and roughly chopped

2 onions, roughly chopped

2 garlic cloves, crushed

115 g/4 oz rindless streaky bacon rashers, roughly chopped

350 g/12 oz/1¾ cups long grain rice

pinch of saffron strands

475 ml/16 fl oz/2 cups vegetable or chicken stock

300 ml/½ pint/1¼ cups dry white wine

350 g/12 oz ripe tomatoes

450 g/1 lb mixed cooked seafood, such as prawns, mussels and squid

115 g/4 oz/1 cup peas, thawed if frozen

45 ml/3 tbsp chopped fresh parsley

salt and freshly ground black pepper

whole cooked prawns and mussels in their shells, to garnish

garlic

tomatoes   *onion*   *red peppers*

mussels   *white wine*   *parsley*

peas   *stock*   *cooked seafood*

prawns   *streaky bacon*   *saffron*   *olive oil*   *long grain rice*

1 Heat half the olive oil in a paella pan or large flameproof casserole. Cook the chopped peppers for about 3 minutes, remove with a slotted spoon and drain on kitchen paper. Add the rest of the oil and cook the onions, garlic and bacon for about 5 minutes, or until the onions have softened slightly, stirring regularly.

2 Add the rice and cook for 1 minute. Stir in the saffron, stock, wine and seasoning. Boil, then simmer, covered, for 12–15 minutes. Stir occasionally.

3 Meanwhile, plunge the tomatoes into a bowl of boiling water, then into cold water and skin them. Quarter the tomatoes and scoop out the seeds. Roughly chop the flesh.

4 When the rice is cooked and most of the liquid has been absorbed, stir the tomatoes, seafood, peas and peppers into the mixture and heat gently, stirring occasionally, for 5 minutes or until piping hot. Stir in the parsley and adjust the seasoning before serving, garnished with the whole cooked prawns and mussels.

Kedgeree

This classic rice recipe makes an ideal breakfast dish on a cold morning.

Serves 6

INGREDIENTS
450 g/1 lb mixed smoked fish
300 ml/¹/₂ pint/1¹/₄ cups milk
200 g/7 oz/1 cup long grain rice
1 slice of lemon
50 g/2 oz/¹/₄ cup butter
5 ml/1 tsp medium curry powder
2.5 ml/¹/₂ tsp freshly grated nutmeg
15 ml/1 tbsp chopped fresh parsley
salt and freshly ground black pepper
flat leaf parsley sprigs, to garnish

TO SERVE
2 hard-boiled eggs, quartered
slices of hot buttered toast

smoked fish

parsley

nutmeg

long grain rice

lemon slice

butter

curry powder

milk

eggs

1 Poach the uncooked smoked fish in milk for 10 minutes or until it flakes (see Cook's Tip). Drain off the milk and flake the fish. Mix with other smoked fish.

2 Cook the rice in boiling water together with a slice of lemon for about 10 minutes until just cooked. Drain well.

COOK'S TIP

You can use a variety of smoked fish. Cod and haddock are cold smoked and must be poached. Mackerel and trout are hot smoked and can be added next. If you are using smoked salmon, it can be added at this second stage even though it is cold smoked.

3 Melt the butter in a large heavy-based saucepan and add the rice and fish. Shake the saucepan to mix all the ingredients together thoroughly.

4 Stir in the curry powder, nutmeg, parsley and seasoning. Serve garnished with sprigs of parsley, quartered eggs and slices of hot buttered toast.

Jambalaya

This Cajun dish comes from the Deep South of the USA. It contains a wonderful combination of rice, meat and fish, with a kick of chilli. If you like really spicy food, add a little more chilli powder.

Serves 6

INGREDIENTS
450 g/1 lb skinless, boneless chicken
    thighs
225 g/8 oz chorizo or spicy sausages
5 celery sticks
1 red pepper, seeded
1 green pepper, seeded
about 30 ml/2 tbsp oil
2 onions, roughly chopped
2 garlic cloves, crushed
10 ml/2 tsp mild chilli powder
2.5 ml/¹/₂ tsp ground ginger
300 g/11 oz/1²/₃ cups long grain rice
900 ml/1¹/₂ pints/3³/₄ cups chicken
    stock
175 g/6 oz peeled cooked prawns
salt and freshly ground black pepper
12 cooked prawns in shells, with
    heads removed, to garnish

peeled
prawns   chorizo   celery

chicken thighs   long grain
                    rice   ground
                                ginger

cooked   oil   chicken
prawns   stock

    garlic   onions

1 Cut the chicken and chorizo or spicy sausages into small, bite-size pieces. Cut the celery and peppers into thin 5 cm/2 in strips and set aside.

2 Heat the oil in a very large frying pan or large saucepan and cook the chicken until golden. Remove with a slotted spoon and drain on kitchen paper. Cook the chorizo for 2 minutes and drain on kitchen paper.

3 Add the celery and peppers and cook for 3–4 minutes, until the vegetables begin to soften and turn golden. Drain on kitchen paper. Add a little more oil to the pan, if needed, and cook the onions and garlic for 3 minutes.

4 Stir in the chilli powder and ginger and cook for a further 1 minute.

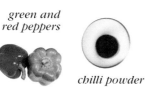

green and
red peppers

chilli powder

5 Add the rice. Cook for 1 minute until it begins to look translucent. Stir in the stock, replace the chicken and bring to the boil. Cover, then simmer for 12–15 minutes, stirring occasionally, until the rice is tender and the liquid has been absorbed. Add a little more water, if necessary, during cooking.

6 Gently stir the chorizo, peppers, celery and peeled prawns into the rice. Cook over a low heat, turning the mixture over with a large spoon, until piping hot. Adjust the seasoning and serve, garnished with the whole prawns.

Middle-eastern Fish with Rice

This Arabic fish dish, *Sayadieh*, is very popular in the Lebanon.

Serves 4-6

INGREDIENTS
juice of 1 lemon
45 ml/3 tbsp oil
900 g/2 lb cod steaks
4 large onions, chopped
5 ml/1 tsp ground cumin
2-3 saffron strands
1 litre/1³⁄₄ pints/4 cups fish stock
450 g/1 lb/2¹⁄₄ cups long grain rice
50 g/2 oz/²⁄₃ cup pine nuts, lightly
    toasted
salt and freshly ground black pepper
fresh parsley, to garnish

lemon   *oil*   *saffron*

onions

cod

long grain rice   *ground cumin*

parsley   *pine nuts*

fish stock

1 Mix together the lemon juice and 15 ml/1 tbsp of the oil in a shallow dish. Add the fish steaks, turning to coat thoroughly, then cover and leave to marinate for 30 minutes. Heat the remaining oil in a large saucepan or flameproof casserole and fry the onions for about 5–6 minutes until golden, stirring occasionally.

2 Drain the fish, reserving the marinade, and add to the pan. Fry for 1–2 minutes each side until lightly golden, then add the cumin, saffron strands and a little salt and pepper.

3 Pour in the fish stock and the reserved marinade and bring to the boil. Leave to simmer gently over a low heat for about 5 minutes until the fish is almost cooked.

VARIATION

You can try this recipe using some other firm-fleshed fish, if you like, such as swordfish. You can also use any type of long grain rice. Brown rice would make a particularly healthy option. If using, add some extra water with the stock and top up if necessary.

4 Transfer the fish to a plate and add the rice to the stock. Bring to the boil and then reduce the heat and simmer gently over a low heat for 15 minutes until the stock has nearly all been absorbed. Add extra water if necessary, a little at a time.

5 Arrange the fish on the rice and cover. Steam over a low heat for a further 10–15 minutes. Transfer the fish to a plate, then spoon the rice on to a large flat dish and arrange the fish on top. Sprinkle with toasted pine nuts and garnish with fresh parsley.

Indonesian Fried Rice

This fried rice dish makes an ideal supper on its own or even as an accompaniment. It is a very quick meal to prepare as the rice is already cooked.

Serves 4

INGREDIENTS
4 shallots, roughly chopped
1 red chilli, seeded and chopped
1 garlic clove, chopped
thin sliver of dried shrimp paste
45 ml/3 tbsp oil
225 g/8 oz boneless lean pork, cut into fine strips
200 g/7 oz/1 cup long grain rice, boiled and cooled
3-4 spring onions, thinly sliced
115 g/4 oz cooked peeled prawns
30 ml/2 tbsp sweet soy sauce
chopped fresh coriander and fine cucumber shreds, to garnish

chilli

shallots

prawns

spring onions

pork

long grain rice

oil

dried shrimp paste

soy sauce

garlic

1 In a mortar pound the shallots, chilli, garlic and shrimp paste with a pestle until they form a paste.

2 Heat a wok until hot, add 30 ml/ 2 tbsp of the oil and swirl it around. Add the pork and stir-fry for 2–3 minutes. Remove the pork from the wok, set aside and keep hot.

3 Add the remaining oil to the wok. When hot, add the spiced shallot paste and stir-fry for about 30 seconds.

4 Reduce the heat. Add the rice, spring onions and prawns. Stir-fry for 2–3 minutes. Add the pork and sprinkle over the soy sauce. Stir-fry until piping hot. Serve garnished with the chopped coriander and cucumber shreds.

Chicken Paella

There are many variations on the basic paella recipe. Any seasonal vegetables can be added, as can mussels and other seafood.

Serves 4

INGREDIENTS

4 chicken legs (thighs and
    drumsticks)
60 ml/4 tbsp olive oil
1 large onion, finely chopped
1 garlic clove, crushed
5 ml/1 tsp ground turmeric
115 g/4 oz chorizo or smoked ham
225 g/8 oz/1¼ cups long
    grain rice
600 ml/1 pint/2½ cups chicken stock
4 tomatoes, peeled, seeded and
    chopped
1 red pepper, seeded and sliced
115 g/4 oz/1 cup frozen peas
salt and freshly ground black pepper

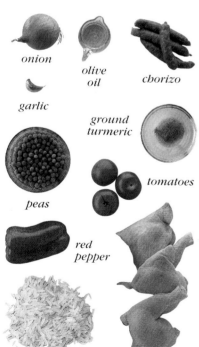

onion

olive
oil

chorizo

garlic

ground
turmeric

peas

tomatoes

red
pepper

long grain rice

chicken

chicken
stock

I Preheat the oven to 180°C/350°F/ Gas 4. Cut the chicken legs in half.

2 Heat the oil in a 30 cm/12 in paella pan or large flameproof casserole and brown the chicken pieces on both sides. Add the onion and garlic and stir in the turmeric. Cook for 2 minutes.

3 Slice the chorizo or dice the ham and add to the pan, together with the rice and stock. Bring to the boil and season to taste. Remove from the hob, cover and bake in the oven for about 15 minutes.

4 Remove from the oven and add the tomatoes, red pepper and frozen peas. Return to the oven and cook for a further 10–15 minutes or until the chicken is tender and the rice has absorbed the stock. Serve hot.

Poussins with Dirty Rice

In this Cajun dish, the rice is called "dirty" not because of its colour but because the local term for jazz is "dirty music", and the rice here will certainly be jazzed up.

Serves 4

INGREDIENTS
60 ml/4 tbsp oil
25 g/1 oz/¼ cup plain flour
50 g/2 oz/¼ cup butter
1 large onion, chopped
2 celery sticks, chopped
1 green pepper, seeded and diced
2 garlic cloves, crushed
200 g/7 oz minced pork
225 g/8 oz chicken livers, trimmed and sliced
dash of Tabasco sauce
300 ml/½ pint/1¼ cups chicken stock
4 spring onions, shredded
45 ml/3 tbsp chopped fresh parsley
225 g/8 oz/1¼ cups long grain rice, freshly cooked
2 bay leaves, halved
4 poussins
25 g/1 oz/2 tbsp butter, for basting
1 lemon
salt and freshly ground black pepper

1 Heat half the oil in a small heavy saucepan and stir in the flour to make a roux. When it is a chestnut-brown colour, remove the pan from the heat and place it immediately on a cold surface. Heat the remaining oil with 50 g/2 oz/¼ cup butter in a frying pan and stir-fry the onion, celery and pepper for 5 minutes.

2 Add the garlic and pork and stir-fry for 5 minutes, breaking up the pork with a spoon so that it cooks evenly. Add the chicken livers and fry for 3 minutes until they have all changed colour. Season and add a dash of Tabasco sauce.

3 Stir the roux into the stir-fried mixture, then gradually add the stock. When the mixture bubbles, cover and simmer for 30 minutes, stirring occasionally. Then uncover and cook for a further 15 minutes, stirring frequently.

4 Preheat the oven to 200°C/400°F/ Gas 6. Mix the spring onions and parsley into the meat mixture and stir it all into the cooked rice. Put ½ bay leaf and about 15 ml/1 tbsp of the rice mixture into each poussin. Rub the outsides with the remaining butter and season well.

oil

flour

butter

Tabasco sauce

garlic

onion

chicken stock

minced pork

celery

bay leaves

chicken livers

green pepper

parsley

spring onions

long grain rice

poussins

lemon

5 Put the birds on a rack in a roasting tin, squeeze the juice from the lemon over them and roast in the oven for 35–40 minutes, basting twice with the pan juices. Put the remaining rice mixture into a shallow ovenproof dish, cover it and place on a low shelf in the oven for the last 15–20 minutes of the birds' cooking time. Serve the birds on a bed of dirty rice with the roasting pan juices (drained of fat) poured over.

COOK'S TIP
You can substitute quails for the poussins, in which case offer two per person and stuff each little bird with 10 ml/2 tsp of the dirty rice before roasting for about 20 minutes.

Thai Fried Rice

This hot and spicy dish is easy to prepare and makes a meal in itself. The delicate balance of flavours is exquisite.

Serves 4

INGREDIENTS

225 g/8 oz/1¼ cups jasmine rice
45 ml/3 tbsp oil
1 onion, chopped
1 small red pepper, seeded and cut into 2 cm/¾ in cubes
350 g/12 oz skinless, boneless chicken breasts, cut into 2 cm/¾ in cubes
1 garlic clove, crushed
15 ml/1 tbsp mild curry paste
2.5 ml/½ tsp paprika
2.5 ml/½ tsp ground turmeric
30 ml/2 tbsp Thai fish sauce (nam pla)
2 eggs, beaten
salt and freshly ground black pepper
fried fresh basil leaves, to garnish

jasmine rice

Thai fish sauce

oil

onion

red pepper

turmeric

curry paste

paprika

garlic

chicken

eggs

1 Place the rice in a sieve and wash well under cold running water. Put the rice in a heavy-based pan with 1.5 litres/2½ pints/6¼ cups boiling water. Return to the boil, then simmer, uncovered, for 8–10 minutes. Drain well. Spread out the grains on a tray and leave to cool.

2 Heat a wok until hot. Add 30 ml/2 tbsp of the oil and swirl it around. Add the onion and red pepper and stir-fry for 1 minute until the onion just begins to soften slightly.

3 Add the chicken, garlic, curry paste and spices and stir-fry for 4–5 minutes, stirring well to evenly distribute the flavours and the paste.

4 Reduce the heat to medium, add the cooled rice, fish sauce and seasoning. Stir-fry for 2–3 minutes until the rice is very hot.

5 Make a well in the centre of the rice and add the remaining oil. When hot, add the beaten eggs, leave to cook for about 2 minutes until lightly set, then stir into the rice.

6 Scatter over the fried basil leaves and serve at once.

VARIATION

Add 50 g/2 oz/¼ cup frozen peas to the chicken in step 3, if you wish.

Chicken Biryani

In India, this dish is mainly prepared for important occasions, and is truly fit for royalty. Every cook has a subtle variation, which is kept a closely guarded secret.

Serves 4-6

INGREDIENTS

1.4 kg/3 lb chicken breast, skinless, boneless, cut into large pieces
60 ml/4 tbsp biryani masala paste
2 green chillies, chopped
15 ml/1 tbsp crushed fresh ginger
4 garlic cloves, crushed
50 g/2 oz fresh coriander, chopped
6-8 fresh mint leaves, chopped or 5 ml/1 tsp mint sauce
150 ml/¼ pint/⅔ cup natural yogurt, beaten
30 ml/2 tbsp tomato purée
4 onions, finely sliced, deep fried and crushed
salt, to taste
450 g/1 lb/2¼ cups basmati rice, washed and drained
5 ml/1 tsp black cumin seeds
1 piece cinnamon stick, 5 cm/2 in long
4 green cardamoms
2 black cardamoms
oil, for shallow frying
4 large potatoes, peeled and quartered
350 ml/12 fl oz/1½ cups mixed milk and water
1 sachet saffron powder, mixed with 90 ml/6 tbsp milk
30 ml/2 tbsp ghee or unsalted butter

FOR THE GARNISH

ghee or unsalted butter, for shallow-frying
50 g/2 oz/½ cup cashew nuts
50 g/2 oz/⅓ cup sultanas
2 hard-boiled eggs, quartered
deep fried onion slices

1 Mix the chicken with the next 10 ingredients in a large bowl and allow to marinate for about 2 hours. Place in a large heavy pan and cook gently for about 10 minutes. Set aside.

2 Bring a large saucepan of water to the boil. Add the rice, cumin seeds, cinnamon stick and cardamoms, remove from the heat and soak for 5 minutes. Drain well. Remove the cinnamon and cardamoms at this stage, if you like.

3 Heat the oil for shallow frying in a frying pan and fry the potatoes until they are evenly browned on all sides. Drain the potatoes on kitchen paper and set aside until needed.

chicken breast

biryani masala paste

chillies

ginger

garlic

coriander

tomato purée

yogurt

mint

saffron

black cumin seeds

basmati rice

cinnamon stick

oil

potatoes

butter

ghee

cardamoms

milk

onions

cashew nuts

sultanas

eggs

4 Place half the rice on top of the chicken mixture in the pan in an even layer. Top with an even layer of potatoes. Put the remaining rice mixture on top of the potatoes and spread out to make an even layer. Sprinkle the milk and water mixture all over the top of the rice.

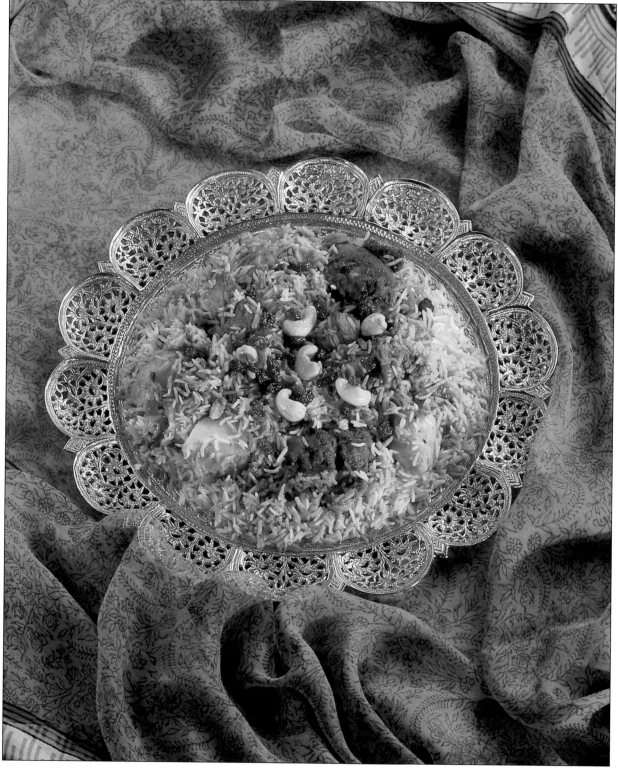

5 Make holes on the top with the handle of a spoon and pour a little saffron milk into each one. Add a few knobs of ghee or butter, cover and cook over a low heat for 35–45 minutes.

6 While the biryani is cooking, make the garnish. Heat a little ghee or butter in a frying pan and fry the cashew nuts and sultanas until the sultanas swell. Drain and set aside. When the biryani is ready, gently toss the rice, chicken and potatoes together. Garnish with the nut mixture, hard-boiled eggs and onion slices and serve hot.

Nasi Goreng

This dish is originally from Thailand, but it can easily be adapted by adding any cooked ingredients that are at hand. Crispy prawn crackers make an ideal accompaniment.

Serves 4

INGREDIENTS
225 g/8 oz/1¼ cups long grain rice
2 eggs
30 ml/2 tbsp oil
1 green chilli
2 spring onions, roughly chopped
2 garlic cloves, crushed
225 g/8 oz cooked chicken
225 g/8 oz cooked prawns, peeled
45 ml/3 tbsp dark soy sauce
spring onion shreds, to garnish
prawn crackers, to serve

long grain rice

eggs

chilli

oil

dark soy sauce

garlic

spring onions

prawns

cooked chicken

1 Rinse and drain the rice and then place in a saucepan together with 600 ml/1 pint/2½ cups water. Bring to the boil, cover with a tight-fitting lid and cook over a low heat for about 10–12 minutes. Rinse the rice with cold water through a sieve to cool it.

2 Lightly beat the eggs. Heat 15 ml/ 1 tbsp of oil in a small frying pan and swirl in the beaten egg. When cooked on one side, flip over and cook on the other side, remove from the pan and leave to cool. Cut the omelette into thin strips and leave aside.

3 Carefully remove the seeds from the chilli and chop finely, wearing rubber gloves to protect your hands if necessary. Always keep hands away from eyes when chopping chillies. Place the spring onions, chilli and garlic in a food processor and blend to a paste.

4 Heat the wok, and then add the remaining oil. When the oil is hot, add the paste and stir-fry for 1 minute.

5 Add the cooked chicken and prawns and stir-fry until hot, making sure that the paste coats the chicken and prawns evenly.

6 Add the cooked rice and stir-fry for 3–4 minutes until piping hot. Stir in the omelette strips and soy sauce and garnish with spring onion shreds. Serve with prawn crackers.

Red Beans and Rice with Salt Pork

This classic Cajun dish is worth making in large quantities because of the long cooking time. It makes a splendid supper-party dish served with grilled sausages and a green salad.

Serves 8-10

INGREDIENTS

500 g/1¼ lb/2 cups dried red kidney beans, soaked in cold water overnight, rinsed and drained
2 bay leaves
30 ml/2 tbsp oil, bacon fat or lard
1 onion, chopped
2 garlic cloves, finely chopped
2 celery sticks, sliced
225 g/8 oz piece of salt pork or raw ham
450 g/1 lb/2¼ cups long grain rice
45 ml/3 tbsp chopped fresh parsley
salt and freshly ground black pepper

red kidney beans

bay leaves

oil

onion

garlic

celery

parsley

long grain rice

ham

1 Place the beans in a large saucepan with cold water to cover. Boil rapidly for 10 minutes. Drain and rinse the beans and the pan. Return the beans to the pan, add the bay leaves and cover with cold water. Bring to the boil, reduce the heat and simmer for 30 minutes.

4 Measure the rice into a pan with a cup and add 750 ml/1¼ pints/3 cups water. Stir in 5 ml/1 tsp salt. Bring to the boil, stirring occasionally, then cover the pan with a tight-fitting lid and leave to cook over a very low heat for about 15 minutes. Without lifting the lid, turn off the heat and leave the rice for a further 5–10 minutes.

COOK'S TIP

Red kidney beans carry dangerous toxins so it is very important that they are washed, soaked overnight and fast boiled before cooking.

2 Meanwhile heat the oil, fat or lard in a frying pan and cook the onion, garlic and celery gently, stirring frequently, until the onion is soft and translucent. Add them to the beans.

5 Lift the piece of salt pork or ham out from among the beans and dice it, removing the fat and rind.

3 Add the piece of salt pork or ham to the beans, pushing well down. Bring back to the boil and simmer, topping up the water as necessary, for 45 minutes until the beans are very tender. Add salt, if necessary, 15–20 minutes before the end of the cooking time.

6 Drain the beans and adjust the seasoning. Mix the meat through the beans. Fluff up the rice and stir in the parsley. Serve with the beans on top.

Lamb Pilau

In the Caribbean rice is often cooked with meat and coconut milk, giving a deliciously rich and creamy texture. Sweet potato crisps would make an ideal accompaniment, and are easily made by deep frying thin slices of the vegetable until crisp.

Serves 4

INGREDIENTS
450 g/1 lb stewing lamb
15 ml/1 tbsp curry powder
1 onion, chopped
2 garlic cloves, crushed
2.5 ml/¹/₂ tsp dried thyme
2.5 ml/¹/₂ tsp dried oregano
1 fresh or dried chilli, seeded and
    chopped
25 g/1 oz/2 tbsp butter or margarine,
    plus extra for serving
600 ml/1 pint/2¹/₂ cups beef or
    chicken stock or coconut milk
5 ml/1 tsp freshly ground black
    pepper
2 tomatoes, chopped
10 ml/2 tsp granulated sugar
30 ml/2 tbsp chopped spring onions
450 g/1 lb/2¹/₄ cups basmati rice
spring onion strips, to garnish

I Cut the meat into cubes, discarding any excess fat and gristle. Place in a shallow glass or china dish.

lamb

curry powder
onion
thyme
oregano

basmati rice

spring onions
butter
stock
sugar

tomatoes
chilli
pepper
garlic

2 Sprinkle with the curry powder, onion, garlic, herbs and chilli. Stir well. Cover loosely with clear film and leave to marinate in a cool place for 1 hour. Melt the butter or margarine in a saucepan and fry the lamb on all sides for 5–10 minutes. Add the stock or coconut milk. Bring to the boil, lower the heat and simmer for 35 minutes or until the meat is tender.

3 Add the black pepper, tomatoes, sugar, spring onions and rice, stir well and reduce the heat. Make sure that the rice is covered by 2.5 cm/1 in of liquid and add a little water if necessary. Simmer the pilau for 25 minutes or until the rice is cooked, then stir a little extra butter or margarine into the rice before serving. Garnish with spring onion strips.

Wild Rice and Turkey Salad

A delicious and healthy salad that makes a perfect light lunch or supper dish. For a softer texture but a similar flavour, use a mixture of wild rice and long grain rice and reduce the cooking time a little.

Serves 4

INGREDIENTS

175 g/6 oz/³/₄ cup wild rice
2 celery stalks, thinly sliced
2 spring onions, chopped
115 g/4 oz/1 cup small button
    mushrooms, quartered
450 g/1 lb cold cooked turkey breast,
    diced
120 ml/4 fl oz/¹/₂ cup vinaigrette
    dressing, made with walnut oil
salt
4 fresh thyme sprigs

TO SERVE

2 pears, peeled, halved and cored
25 g/1 oz/3 tbsp walnut pieces,
    toasted

1 Pour 1 litre/1³/₄ pints/4 cups cold water into a saucepan and add a pinch of salt. Bring to the boil. Add the wild rice to the pan and bring back to the boil. Cook for 45–50 minutes, until tender but firm and the grains have begun to split open. Drain well and leave to cool.

 celery

wild rice

pears

thyme

turkey breast

spring onions

walnut pieces

mushrooms

VARIATION

You can use chicken instead of turkey breast with any vinaigrette dressing. Toast a selection of nuts for a different flavour, if you like.

2 Combine the wild rice with the celery, spring onions, mushrooms and cooked turkey in a bowl.

3 Add the dressing and thyme and toss well together. Thinly slice the pear halves lengthways without cutting through the stalk end and spread the slices like a fan. Divide the salad among 4 plates. Garnish each with a fanned pear half and toasted walnuts.

Oriental Fried Rice

This is a great way to use leftover cooked rice.
Make sure the rice is very cold before attempting
to fry it as warm rice will become soggy. Some
supermarkets sell frozen cooked rice.

Serves 4-6

INGREDIENTS
75 ml/5 tbsp oil
115 g/4 oz shallots, halved and thinly
   sliced
3 garlic cloves, crushed
1 red chilli, seeded and finely
   chopped
6 spring onions, finely chopped
1 red pepper, seeded and finely
   chopped
225 g/8 oz white cabbage, finely
   shredded
175 g/6 oz cucumber, finely chopped
50 g/2 oz/¹⁄₂ cup peas, thawed if
   frozen
3 eggs, beaten
5 ml/1 tsp tomato purée
30 ml/2 tbsp lime juice
1.5 ml/¹⁄₄ tsp Tabasco sauce
225 g/8 oz/1¹⁄₄ cups long grain rice,
   cooked and cooled
115 g/4 oz/1 cup cashew nuts,
   roughly chopped
about 30 ml/2 tbsp chopped fresh
   coriander, plus extra to garnish
salt and freshly ground black pepper

1 Heat half the oil in a large non-stick frying pan or wok and cook the shallots until very crisp and golden. Remove with a slotted spoon and drain well on kitchen paper.

2 Add the rest of the oil to the pan. Cook the garlic and chilli for 1 minute. Add the spring onions and pepper and cook for a further 3–4 minutes.

3 Add the cabbage, cucumber and peas and cook for a further 2 minutes.

red pepper

white cabbage

red chilli

spring onions

coriander

garlic

shallots

oil

Tabasco sauce

cucumber

eggs

lime juice

peas

cashew nuts

long grain rice

tomato purée

4 Make a gap in the pan and add the beaten eggs. Scramble the eggs, stirring occasionally, and then stir them into the vegetables.

5 Add the tomato purée, lime juice and Tabasco and stir to combine.

6 Increase the heat and add the rice, cashew nuts and coriander with plenty of seasoning. Stir-fry for 3–4 minutes, until piping hot. Serve garnished with the crisp shallots and extra fresh coriander.

Lentils and Rice

Lentils are cooked with whole and ground spices, potatoes, rice and onions here to produce an authentic Indian-style dish, which makes a satisfying light but wholesome meal.

Serves 4

INGREDIENTS
150 g/5 oz/²⁄₃ cup red split lentils
115 g/4 oz/²⁄₃ cup basmati rice
1 large potato
1 large onion
30 ml/2 tbsp oil
4 whole cloves
1.5 ml/¼ tsp cumin seeds
1.5 ml/¼ tsp ground turmeric
10 ml/2 tsp salt

basmati rice

oil

cumin seeds

ground turmeric

red split lentils

potato

salt

cloves   *onion*

1 Wash the lentils and rice in several changes of cold water. Place in a bowl and cover with water. Leave to soak for 15 minutes, then drain.

2 While the rice and lentils are soaking, peel the potato and rinse well. Cut it into 2.5 cm/1 in chunks. Peel the onion and cut the onion into thin slices.

3 Heat the oil in a large heavy-based saucepan and fry the cloves and cumin seeds for 2 minutes until the seeds are beginning to splutter.

4 Add the onion and potatoes and fry for 5 minutes until slightly browned. Add the lentils and rice, with turmeric and salt and fry for 3 minutes.

5 Pour 475 ml/16 fl oz/2 cups water into a saucepan. Bring to the boil, cover tightly and simmer for 15–20 minutes, until all the water has been absorbed and the potatoes are tender. Leave to stand, covered, for about 10 minutes, and then serve.

Vegetable Kedgeree

Crunchy French beans and mushrooms are the star
ingredients in this vegetarian version of a rice dish
traditionally made with fish as well as egg.

Serves 2

INGREDIENTS
115 g/4 oz/²⁄₃ cup basmati rice
3 eggs
175 g/6 oz French beans, trimmed
50 g/2 oz/4 tbsp butter
1 onion, finely chopped
225 g/8 oz/2 cups brown cap
    mushrooms, quartered
30 ml/2 tbsp single cream
15 ml/1 tbsp chopped fresh parsley
salt and freshly ground black pepper

basmati
rice

single
cream

French
beans

butter

onion

parsley

brown cap
mushrooms

1 Wash the rice several times under
cold running water. Drain thoroughly.
Bring a pan of water to the boil, add the
rice and cook for 10–12 minutes until
tender. Drain thoroughly.

2 Half fill a second pan with water,
add the eggs and bring to the boil.
Lower the heat and simmer for
8 minutes. Drain the eggs, cool them
under running cold water, then remove
the shells and rinse.

3 Bring another pan of water to the
boil and cook the French beans for
about 5 minutes. Drain, refresh under
cold running water, then drain again.

4 Melt the butter in a large frying pan.
Add the onion and mushrooms. Cook
for 2–3 minutes over a moderate heat.

5 Add the French beans and rice to
the onion mixture. Stir lightly to mix.
Cook for 2 minutes. Cut the hard-boiled
eggs in wedges and carefully add them
to the pan.

6 Stir in the cream and parsley, taking
care not to break up the eggs. Reheat
the kedgeree, but do not allow it to boil.
Season with salt and pepper and serve
at once.

Vegetable Pilau

A delicious vegetable rice dish that also goes well
with most Indian meat dishes.

Serves 4-6

INGREDIENTS

225 g/8 oz/1¼ cups basmati rice
30 ml/2 tbsp oil
2.5 ml/½ tsp cumin seeds
2 bay leaves
4 green cardamom pods
4 cloves
1 onion, finely chopped
1 carrot, finely chopped
50 g/2 oz/½ cup peas, thawed if
　frozen
50 g/2 oz/⅓ cup sweetcorn kernels,
　thawed if frozen
25 g/1 oz/¼ cup cashew nuts, lightly
　fried
1.5 ml/¼ tsp ground coriander
1.5 ml/¼ tsp ground cumin
salt

ground
coriander

peas

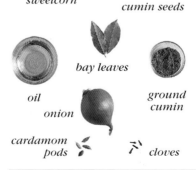

sweetcorn

carrot

cumin seeds

bay leaves

oil

onion

ground
cumin

cardamom
pods

cloves

cashew
nuts

basmati
rice

1 Wash the basmati rice in several
changes of cold water. Put into a bowl
and cover with cold water. Leave to
soak for 30 minutes.

2 Heat the oil in a large frying pan and
fry the cumin seeds for 2 minutes. Add
the bay leaves, cardamoms and cloves
and fry for 2 minutes.

3 Add the onion and fry for 5 minutes
until lightly browned.

4 Stir in the carrot and cook for
3–4 minutes.

5 Drain the rice and add to the pan
with the peas, sweetcorn and cashew
nuts. Fry for 4–5 minutes.

VARIATION

You can add your favourite
vegetables to this recipe, such as
potatoes, if you like, although this
particular vegetable will require a
longer cooking time.

6 Pour in 475 ml/16 fl oz/2 cups cold
water, then add the remaining spices
and salt to taste. Bring to the boil, cover,
then simmer for about 15 minutes over
a low heat until all the water is
absorbed. Leave to stand, covered, for
10 minutes before serving.

Stuffed Vegetables

Vegetables such as peppers make wonderful containers for savoury fillings. Instead of sticking to one type of vegetable serve a selection. Thick, creamy Greek yogurt is the ideal accompaniment.

Serves 3-6

INGREDIENTS
1 aubergine
1 large green pepper
2 large tomatoes
1 large onion, chopped
2 garlic cloves, crushed
45 ml/3 tbsp olive oil
200 g/7 oz/1 cup brown rice
600 ml/1 pint/2½ cups vegetable
    stock
75 g/3 oz/1 cup pine nuts
50 g/2 oz/⅓ cup currants
45 ml/3 tbsp chopped fresh dill
45 ml/3 tbsp chopped fresh parsley
15 ml/1 tbsp chopped fresh mint
extra olive oil, to sprinkle
salt and freshly ground black pepper
Greek yogurt and fresh dill sprigs,
    to serve

aubergine   *garlic*   *tomatoes*   *yogurt*

green pepper   *onion*

olive oil   *brown rice*   *pine nuts*   *vegetable stock*

dill   *parsley*   *mint*   *currants*

1 Halve the aubergine, scoop out the flesh with a sharp knife and chop finely. Salt the insides and leave to drain upside down for 20 minutes while you prepare the other ingredients. Halve the pepper, seed and core.

2 Cut the tops from the tomatoes, scoop out the insides and chop roughly along with the tomato tops. Set the tomato shells aside. Fry the onion, garlic and chopped aubergine in the oil for 10 minutes, then stir in the rice and cook for 2 minutes. Add the tomato flesh, stock, pine nuts, currants and seasoning. Bring to the boil, cover and lower the heat. Simmer for 15 minutes then stir in the herbs.

3 Preheat the oven to 190°C/375°F/ Gas 5. Blanch the aubergine and green pepper halves in boiling water for about 3 minutes, then drain them upside down on kitchen paper.

4 Spoon the rice filling into all six vegetable containers and place on a lightly greased shallow baking dish. Drizzle some olive oil over the stuffed vegetables and bake for 25–30 minutes. Serve hot, topped with spoonfuls of yogurt and the dill sprigs.

Pilau with Omelette Rolls and Nuts

A wonderful mixture of textures – soft fluffy rice with crunchy nuts and omelette rolls.

Serves 2

INGREDIENTS
175 g/6 oz/scant 1 cup basmati rice
15 ml/1 tbsp sunflower oil
1 small onion, chopped
1 red pepper, finely diced
350 ml/12 fl oz/1½ cups hot
    vegetable stock
2 eggs
25 g/1 oz/¼ cup salted peanuts
15 ml/1 tbsp soy sauce
salt and freshly ground black pepper
fresh parsley sprigs, to garnish

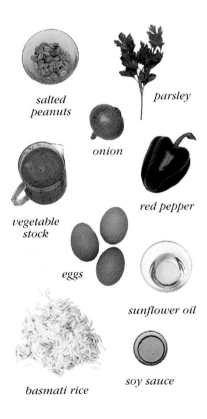

salted peanuts

parsley

onion

red pepper

vegetable stock

eggs

sunflower oil

soy sauce

basmati rice

1 Wash the rice several times under cold running water. Drain thoroughly. Heat half the oil in a large frying pan. Fry the onion and pepper for 2–3 minutes, then stir in the rice and stock, bring to the boil and cook for 10–12 minutes until the rice is tender.

2 Meanwhile, beat the eggs lightly with salt and pepper to taste. Heat the remaining oil in a second large frying pan. Pour in the eggs and tilt the pan to cover the base thinly. Cook the omelette for 1 minute, then flip it over and cook the other side for 1 minute.

3 Slide the omelette on to a clean board and roll it up tightly. Cut the omelette roll into 8 slices.

4 Stir the peanuts and the soy sauce into the pilau and add black pepper to taste. Turn the pilau into a serving dish, arrange the omelette rolls on top and garnish with the parsley. Serve at once.

Fruity Rice Salad

An appetizing and colourful rice salad combining many different flavours, ideal for a packed lunch.

Serves 4-6

INGREDIENTS
225 g/8 oz/1 cup mixed brown and
 wild rice
1 yellow pepper, seeded and diced
1 bunch spring onions, chopped
3 celery sticks, chopped
1 large beefsteak tomato, chopped
2 green-skinned eating apples,
 chopped
175 g/6 oz/³/₄ cup ready-to-eat dried
 apricots, chopped
115 g/4 oz/²/₃ cup raisins

FOR THE DRESSING
30 ml/2 tbsp unsweetened apple
 juice
30 ml/2 tbsp dry sherry
30 ml/2 tbsp light soy sauce
dash of Tabasco sauce
30 ml/2 tbsp chopped fresh parsley
15 ml/1 tbsp chopped fresh rosemary
salt and freshly ground black pepper

celery

mixed brown
and wild rice

spring
onions

beefsteak
tomato

apricots

apple juice

soy sauce

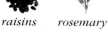
raisins

rosemary

parsley

sherry

Tabasco
sauce

eating
apples

yellow
pepper

1 Cook the rice in a large saucepan of lightly salted, boiling water for about 35 minutes until tender. Rinse the rice under cold running water to cool quickly and drain thoroughly.

2 Place the pepper, spring onions, celery, tomato, apples, apricots, raisins and the cooked rice in a large serving bowl and mix well.

3 To make the dressing, mix together the apple juice, sherry, soy sauce, Tabasco sauce, fresh herbs and seasoning in a small bowl.

4 Pour the dressing over the rice mixture and toss the ingredients together to mix. Serve immediately or cover and chill in the fridge until ready to serve.

Risotto with Asparagus

A fresh and delicious risotto is one of the nicest classic rice dishes. This recipe makes an elegant meal when asparagus is in season.

Serves 4-5

INGREDIENTS

225 g/8 oz asparagus, lower stalks
   peeled
750 ml/1¼ pints/3 cups vegetable or
   meat stock, preferably home-made
65 g/2½ oz/5 tbsp butter
1 small onion, finely chopped
400 g/14 oz/2 cups risotto rice
75 g/3 oz/1 cup freshly grated
   Parmesan cheese
salt and freshly ground black pepper

asparagus

stock

butter

risotto rice

onion

Parmesan
cheese

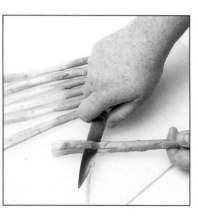

1 Boil 750 ml/1¼ pints/3 cups water in a large saucepan and blanch the asparagus for 5 minutes. Remove, reserving the cooking water and rinse under cold water. Drain and cut each one diagonally into 4 cm/1½ in pieces, separating the tip and next-highest sections from the stalks. Place the stock in a saucepan with 600 ml/1 pint/2½ cups of the asparagus cooking water. Heat the liquid to simmering, and keep it hot until it is needed.

2 Heat two-thirds of the butter in a large heavy frying pan or casserole. Add the onion and cook until it is soft and golden. Stir in the asparagus stalks. Cook for 2–3 minutes. Add the rice, mixing well to coat the grains with butter. Cook for 1–2 minutes.

3 Stir in half a ladleful of the hot liquid. Stir constantly until the liquid has been absorbed. Add another half ladleful of the liquid, and stir until it has also been absorbed. Continue stirring and adding the liquid, a little at a time, for about 10 minutes.

COOK'S TIP

Parmesan cheese is ideal for cooking because it does not become stringy or rubbery when heated. It can be grated over many hot dishes, such as pasta and risotto, as well as added to cold salads. There are two basic types of Parmesan cheeses – Parmigiano Reggiano and Grana Padano – but the former is superior in quality.

4 Add the remaining asparagus sections, and continue cooking, stirring and adding the liquid until the rice is *al dente*. Total cooking time will be about 30 minutes. If you run out of stock, use hot water, but do not worry if the rice is ready before all the stock has been added. Remove the pan from the heat and stir in the remaining butter and the Parmesan. Add a little black pepper and salt to taste. Serve at once.

Risotto-stuffed Aubergines with Spicy Tomato Sauce

Aubergines are a challenge to the creative cook and allow for some unusual recipe ideas. Here, they are stuffed and baked with a cheese and pine nut topping.

COOK'S TIP

If the aubergine shells do not stand level, cut a thin slice from the base. When browning the filled shells, use crumpled foil to support them.

Serves 4

INGREDIENTS
4 small aubergines
105 ml/7 tbsp olive oil
1 small onion, chopped
175 g/6 oz/scant 1 cup risotto rice
750 ml/1¼ pints/3 cups hot
    vegetable stock
15 ml/1 tbsp white wine vinegar
25 g/1 oz/⅓ cup freshly grated
    Parmesan cheese
15 g/½ oz/2 tbsp pine nuts
8 fresh basil sprigs, to garnish

FOR THE TOMATO SAUCE
300 ml/½ pint/1¼ cups thick passata
    or tomato purée
5 ml/1 tsp mild curry paste
pinch of salt

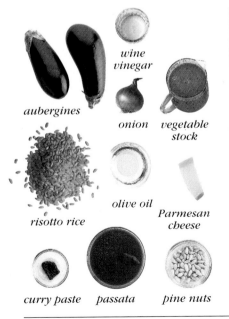

aubergines

wine vinegar

onion *vegetable stock*

risotto rice

olive oil

Parmesan cheese

curry paste *passata* *pine nuts*

1 Preheat the oven to 200°C/400°F/ Gas 6. Cut the aubergines in half lengthways and take out their flesh with a small knife. Brush the shells with 30 ml/2 tbsp of the oil, place on a baking sheet and bake for 6–8 minutes.

2 Chop the reserved aubergine flesh. Heat the remainder of the olive oil in a medium saucepan. Add the aubergine flesh and the onion and cook over a gentle heat for about 3–4 minutes until just soft.

3 Add the rice, stir in the stock and leave to simmer uncovered for a further 15 minutes. Stir in the vinegar.

4 Increase the oven temperature to 230°C/450°F/Gas 8. Spoon the rice into the aubergine skins, top with the cheese and pine nuts, return to the oven and brown for 5 minutes.

5 To make the sauce, mix the passata or tomato purée with the curry paste in a small pan. Heat through and add salt to taste.

6 Spoon the sauce on to four large serving plates and position two stuffed aubergine halves on each. Garnish with basil sprigs.

Leek, Mushroom and Lemon Risotto

A delicious risotto, packed full of flavour makes a marvellous treat for friends or family.

Serves 4

INGREDIENTS

225 g/8 oz trimmed leeks
225 g/8 oz/2–3 cups brown cap
  mushrooms
30 ml/2 tbsp olive oil
3 garlic cloves, crushed
75 g/3 oz/6 tbsp butter
1 large onion, roughly chopped
350 g/12 oz/1¾ cups risotto rice
1.2 litres/2 pints/5 cups simmering
  vegetable stock
grated rind of 1 lemon
45 ml/3 tbsp lemon juice
50 g/2 oz/⅔ cup freshly grated
  Parmesan cheese
60 ml/4 tbsp mixed chopped fresh
  chives and flat leaf parsley
salt and freshly ground black pepper
lemon wedges, to serve

leeks

mushrooms

olive oil

lemon

butter

risotto rice

onion

Parmesan cheese

garlic

vegetable stock

parsley

chives

1 Wash the leeks well. Slice them in half lengthways and chop them roughly. Wipe the mushrooms with kitchen paper and chop them roughly.

2 Heat the oil in a large saucepan and cook the garlic for 1 minute. Add the leeks, mushrooms and plenty of seasoning and cook over a medium heat for about 10 minutes, or until softened and browned. Remove from the pan and set aside.

3 Add 25 g/1 oz of the butter to the pan. As soon as it has melted, add the onion and cook over a medium heat for 5 minutes until softened and golden.

4 Stir in the rice and cook for about 1 minute until the grains begin to look translucent and are coated in the fat. Add a ladleful of stock to the pan and cook gently, stirring occasionally, until the liquid has been absorbed.

5 Continue to add stock, a ladleful at a time, until all the stock has been absorbed. This should take about 25–30 minutes. The risotto will turn thick and creamy and the rice should be tender but not sticky.

6 Just before serving, stir in the leeks, mushrooms, remaining butter, grated lemon rind and juice. Add half the grated Parmesan and herbs. Adjust the seasoning and serve, sprinkled with the remaining Parmesan, herbs and lemon wedges. Garnish with parsley, if you like.

Shellfish Risotto with Mixed Mushrooms

The combination of shellfish and mushrooms in this creamy risotto is exquisite. Serve with chunks of hot ciabatta, if you like.

Serves 4

INGREDIENTS

225 g/8 oz live mussels
225 g/8 oz Venus or carpet shell
   clams
45 ml/3 tbsp olive oil
1 onion, chopped
225 g/8 oz/2-3 cups assorted wild
   and cultivated mushrooms,
   trimmed and sliced
450 g/1 lb/2¼ cups risotto rice
1.2 litres/2 pints/5 cups hot chicken
   or vegetable stock
150 ml/¼ pint/⅔ cup white wine
115 g/4 oz cooked prawns, deveined,
   heads and tails removed
1 squid, cleaned, trimmed and sliced
3 drops truffle oil (optional)
75 ml/5 tbsp chopped fresh parsley
   and chervil
celery salt and cayenne pepper

olive oil
mushrooms
white wine
risotto rice
stock
onion
parsley
prawns
mussels
clams
truffle oil
squid

1 Scrub the mussels and clams clean and tap them with a knife. If any shells do not close, discard them. Put aside. Heat the oil in a large saucepan and fry the onion for 6–8 minutes until soft but not browned.

COOK'S TIP

Use a mixture of mushrooms, such as ceps, bay boletus, chanterelles, chicken of the woods, saffron milk-caps, horn of plenty, wood blewits, oyster, St George's, Caesar's and truffles. Wash all mushrooms carefully, particularly wild ones. It is worth noting that chicken of the woods mushrooms may need blanching in boiling salted water for 2–3 minutes before cooking, to remove their slight bitter taste. Also, use truffles sparingly, as they have a strong flavour.

2 Add the mushrooms and allow them to soften, until their juices begin to run. Stir in the rice and heat through.

3 Pour in the stock and wine. Add the prawns, mussels, clams and squid, stir gently and simmer for 15 minutes. If any of the mussels and clams do not open after cooking, discard them.

4 Remove from the heat. Add the truffle oil if using, and stir in the herbs. Cover tightly and leave to stand for 5–10 minutes to allow all the flavours to blend. Season to taste with celery salt and a pinch of cayenne pepper and serve immediately.

Salmon Risotto with Cucumber and Tarragon

Arborio or carnaroli rices are ideal for this simple and delicious risotto. Fresh tarragon and cucumber combine well in this recipe to bring out the flavour of the salmon, making a particularly delicate and fragrant dish.

Serves 4

INGREDIENTS

25 g/1 oz/2 tbsp butter
1 small bunch of spring onions, white
    parts only, chopped
½ cucumber, peeled, seeded and
    chopped
400 g/14 oz/2 cups risotto rice
900 ml/1½ pints/3¾ cups chicken or
    fish stock
150 ml/¼ pint/⅔ cup dry white wine
450 g/1 lb salmon fillet, skinned and
    diced
45 ml/3 tbsp chopped fresh tarragon

1 Heat the butter in a large saucepan and add the spring onions and cucumber. Cook for 2–3 minutes without colouring.

butter

stock

spring onions

salmon fillet

white wine

cucumber

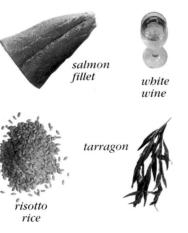
risotto rice

tarragon

VARIATION

Smoked salmon can be used instead of fresh. Buy offcuts, which are cheaper than slices, and cut them into bite-size pieces. Add right at the end, just before the standing time.

2 Add the rice, stock and wine, return to the boil and simmer uncovered for 10 minutes, stirring occasionally.

3 Stir in the diced salmon and tarragon. Continue cooking for a further 5 minutes, then switch off the heat. Cover and leave to stand for 5 minutes before serving.

Risotto with Chicken

A classic combination of chicken and rice, cooked with Parma ham, white wine and Parmesan.

Serves 4

INGREDIENTS

30 ml/2 tbsp olive oil
225 g/8 oz skinless, boneless chicken
    breast, cut into 2.5 cm/1 in cubes
1 onion, finely chopped
1 garlic clove, finely chopped
1.5 ml/^{1}/$_4$ tsp saffron strands
50 g/2 oz Parma ham, cut into thin
    strips
450 g/1 lb/2^1/$_4$ cups risotto rice
120 ml/4 fl oz/^{1}/$_2$ cup dry white wine
1.75 litres/3 pints/7^1/$_2$ cups
    simmering chicken stock
25 g/1 oz/2 tbsp butter (optional)
25 g/1 oz/^{1}/$_3$ cup freshly grated
    Parmesan cheese, plus more
    to serve
salt and freshly ground black pepper
flat leaf parsley, to garnish

olive oil · onion · garlic · saffron · chicken · risotto rice · stock · white wine · Parma ham · butter · Parmesan cheese · parsley

1 Heat the oil in a wide heavy-based pan over moderately high heat. Add the chicken cubes and cook, stirring, until they start to turn white.

2 Reduce the heat to low and add the onion, garlic, saffron and Parma ham. Cook, stirring, until the onion is soft. Stir in the rice. Sauté for 1–2 minutes, stirring constantly.

3 Add the wine and bring to the boil. Simmer gently until almost all the wine has been absorbed. Add the simmering stock, a ladleful at a time, until absorbed and cook until the rice is just tender and the risotto is creamy.

4 Add the butter, if using, and the Parmesan cheese and stir in well. Season with salt and pepper to taste. Serve the risotto hot, sprinkled with a little more Parmesan, and garnish with parsley.

Risotto with Smoky Bacon and Tomato

A classic risotto, with plenty of onions, smoked bacon and sun-dried tomatoes. You'll want to keep going back for more!

Serves 4

INGREDIENTS

8 sun-dried tomatoes in olive oil
275 g/10 oz good-quality rindless
   smoked back bacon
75 g/3 oz/6 tbsp butter
450 g/1 lb onions, roughly chopped
2 garlic cloves, crushed
350 g/12 oz/1³/₄ cups risotto rice
300 ml/¹/₂ pint/1¹/₄ cups dry white
   wine
900 ml/1¹/₂ pints/3³/₄ cups simmering
   vegetable stock
50 g/2 oz/²/₃ cup freshly grated
   Parmesan cheese
45 ml/3 tbsp mixed chopped fresh
   chives and flat leaf parsley
salt and freshly ground black pepper
flat leaf parsley sprigs, to garnish
lemon wedges, to serve

flat leaf parsley

smoked bacon

chives

vegetable stock

butter

garlic

Parmesan cheese

sun-dried tomatoes

white wine

risotto rice

onions

lemon

1 Drain the sun-dried tomatoes and reserve 15 ml/1 tbsp of the oil. Roughly chop the tomatoes and set aside. Cut the bacon into 2.5 cm/1 in strips.

2 Heat the reserved sun-dried tomato oil in a large saucepan. Fry the bacon until well cooked and golden. Remove with a slotted spoon and drain on kitchen paper.

3 Add 25 g/1 oz/2 tbsp of the butter to the pan. When it melts add the onions and garlic. Cook over a medium heat for 10 minutes, until softened and golden brown.

4 Stir in the rice. Cook for 1 minute until turning translucent. Stir the wine into the simmering stock. Add a ladleful to the rice and cook gently until absorbed.

5 Stir in another ladleful of the stock and wine mixture and allow it to be absorbed again. Repeat this process until all the liquid is used up. This should take 25–30 minutes. The risotto will turn thick and creamy, and the rice should be tender but not sticky.

6 Just before serving, stir in the bacon, sun-dried tomatoes, half the Parmesan and herbs, and the remaining butter. Adjust the seasoning (remember that the bacon may be quite salty) and serve sprinkled with the remaining Parmesan and herbs. Garnish with parsley and serve with lemon wedges.

SIDE DISHES

Egg Fried Rice

This is perhaps one of the most famous of side dishes. Use rice with a fairly firm texture. Ideally, the rice should be soaked in water for a short time before cooking.

Serves 4

INGREDIENTS

3 eggs
5 ml/1 tsp salt
2 spring onions, finely chopped
30-45 ml/2-3 tbsp oil
175 g/6 oz/scant 1 cup long grain rice, cooked and cooled
115 g/4 oz/1 cup peas, thawed if frozen

spring onions

peas

eggs

long grain rice

oil

salt

1 In a bowl, lightly beat the eggs with a pinch of the salt and a few pieces of the chopped spring onions. Heat a wok and when it is hot add some oil. When the oil is hot add the eggs and lightly scramble them.

2 Add the cooked rice and stir to make sure that each grain of rice stays separate. Add the remaining salt, spring onions and the peas. Mix well and stir-fry for a few minutes, until the rice is piping hot. Serve immediately.

Coconut Rice

This side dish is popular in Thailand, where jasmine rice is commonly eaten and coconut is used in many recipes. Rich and delicious, this tastes great with a tangy papaya salad.

Serves 4-6

INGREDIENTS

450 g/1 lb/2¼ cups jasmine rice
475 ml/16 fl oz/2 cups coconut milk
2.5 ml/½ tsp salt
30 ml/2 tbsp sugar
fresh shredded coconut, to garnish (optional)

fresh coconut

salt

jasmine rice

sugar

coconut milk

1 Wash the rice in several changes of cold water until it runs clear. Place the coconut milk, salt and sugar in a heavy-bottomed saucepan. Add 250 ml/8 fl oz/ 1 cup water and stir in the rice. Cover and bring to the boil. Reduce the heat and simmer for 15–20 minutes or until the rice is *al dente*.

2 Turn off the heat, cover and allow the rice to rest in the saucepan for a further 5–10 minutes. Fluff up the rice with chopsticks before serving. Garnish with shredded coconut, if you like.

Special Fried Rice

Special Fried Rice is a very popular rice recipe in China. As it contains prawns and ham, it can almost make a meal in itself.

Serves 4

INGREDIENTS

50 g/2 oz cooked prawns, peeled
50 g/2 oz cooked ham
3 eggs
5 ml/1 tsp salt
2 spring onions, finely chopped, plus extra to garnish
60 ml/4 tbsp oil
115 g/4 oz/1 cup peas, thawed if frozen
15 ml/1 tbsp light soy sauce
15 ml/1 tbsp Chinese rice wine or dry sherry
175 g/6 oz/scant 1 cup long grain rice, cooked

prawns

ham

eggs

spring onions

long grain rice

peas

oil

soy sauce

salt

sherry

1 Pat the cooked prawns dry with kitchen paper, making sure no moisture remains. Cut the ham into small dice about the same size as the peas.

2 In a bowl, lightly beat the eggs with a pinch of the salt and a few pieces of the chopped spring onions, using chopsticks or a fork.

COOK'S TIP
Chinese rice wine can be found in Chinese supermarkets and ethnic food shops.

3 Heat the wok, add about half of the oil and when it is hot, stir-fry the peas, prawns and ham for about 1 minute. Add the soy sauce and rice wine or sherry. Transfer the mixture to a dish and keep hot.

4 Heat the remaining oil in the wok and scramble the eggs lightly. Add the rice and stir to separate the grains. Add the remaining salt and spring onions and the prawn mixture. Stir well and heat until the rice is piping hot. Garnish with chopped spring onions.

Long Grain and Wild Rice Ring

This American-style side dish combines two types of rice with currants and onion, to give an unusual texture and delicious flavour.

Serves 8

INGREDIENTS

30 ml/2 tbsp corn oil, plus extra for
    greasing mould
1 large onion, chopped
400 g/14 oz/2 cups mixed long grain
    and wild rice
1.2 litres/2 pints/5 cups chicken
    stock
50 g/2 oz/⅓ cup currants
salt
6 spring onions, cut diagonally into
    5 mm/¼ in pieces
fresh parsley sprigs, to garnish

corn oil

spring onions

onion

chicken stock

parsley

mixed long grain and wild rice

currants

1 Lightly oil a 1.75 litre/3 pint/7½ cup ring mould. Set aside. Heat the oil in a large saucepan. Add the onion and cook for 5 minutes, or until softened.

2 Add the rice to the pan and stir well to coat the rice with the oil.

3 Stir in the chicken stock and bring to the boil. Reduce the heat to low. Stir the currants into the rice mixture. Add salt to taste. Cover and simmer until the rice is tender and the stock has been absorbed, about 35 minutes. Drain the rice if necessary and transfer it to a mixing bowl. Stir in the spring onions.

4 Pack the rice mixture into the prepared mould. Turn it on to a warmed serving platter. Place parsley sprigs in the centre of the ring before serving.

COOK'S TIP

Wild rice needs quite a lengthy cooking time and so you will need a particularly large amount of water for boiling it in. It will, however, need a shorter cooking time if mixed with a long grain rice. Wild rice is ready when the grains have begun to burst open, releasing their nutty aroma.

Okra Fried Rice

If you like hot food, you'll love this spicy vegetable Caribbean speciality.

Serves 3-4

INGREDIENTS

150 g/5 oz okra
30 ml/2 tbsp oil
15 g/½ oz/1 tbsp butter or margarine
1 garlic clove, crushed
½ red onion, finely chopped
30 ml/2 tbsp diced green and red
   peppers
2.5 ml/½ tsp dried thyme
2 green chillies, finely chopped
2.5 ml/½ tsp five-spice powder
½ vegetable stock cube
30 ml/2 tbsp soy sauce
15 ml/1 tbsp chopped fresh
   coriander
175 g/6 oz/scant 1 cup long grain
   rice, cooked
freshly ground black pepper
fresh coriander sprigs, to garnish

oil

butter

red onion

green and red peppers

stock cube

garlic

thyme

okra

green chillies

five-spice powder

soy sauce

coriander

long grain rice

1 Wash and dry the okra, remove the tops and tails and slice thinly and diagonally. Set aside until needed.

2 Heat the oil and butter or margarine in a frying pan or wok, add the garlic and onion and cook over a moderate heat for 5 minutes until soft. Add the sliced okra and sauté gently for 6–7 minutes.

3 Add the green and red peppers, thyme, chillies and five-spice powder and cook for 3 minutes.

4 Crumble in the stock cube, add the soy sauce, coriander and rice and toss over the heat until the rice is piping hot. Add some freshly ground pepper. Serve, garnished with the coriander sprigs.

Pilau Rice Flavoured with Whole Spices

This fragrant rice dish will make a perfect accompaniment to any Indian meal.

Serves 4-6

INGREDIENTS

generous pinch of saffron strands
600 ml/1 pint/2½ cups hot chicken
stock
50 g/2 oz/¼ cup butter
1 onion, chopped
1 garlic clove, crushed
½ cinnamon stick
6 green cardamoms
1 bay leaf
250 g/9 oz/1⅓ cup basmati rice,
rinsed and drained
50 g/2 oz/⅓ cup sultanas
15 ml/1 tbsp oil
50 g/2 oz/½ cup cashew nuts

saffron   chicken   cinnamon
           stock   stick

onion   bay leaf   butter

oil   garlic   cashew nuts

sultanas   cardamoms basmati
                      rice

1 Add the saffron strands to the hot stock and set aside. Heat the butter in a large saucepan and fry the onion and garlic for 5 minutes. Stir in the cinnamon stick, cardamoms and bay leaf and cook for 2 minutes.

2 Add the rice and cook, stirring, for 2 minutes more. Pour in the stock and saffron mixture and add the sultanas. Bring to the boil, stir, then lower the heat. Cover the pan and leave to cook gently for about 15 minutes or until the rice is tender and all the liquid has been absorbed.

3 Meanwhile, heat the oil in a wok or frying pan and fry the cashew nuts until browned. Drain on kitchen paper. Scatter over the rice and serve.

VARIATION

You can add a mixture of nuts to this recipe, if you like, such as almonds, peanuts or hazelnuts. Some nuts may be bought complete with their brown, papery skins, which should be removed before use. The flavour of all nuts is improved by toasting.

COOK'S TIP

Remember to keep all spices stored in separate airtight containers. This helps them to retain their flavour as well as preventing their aromas from spreading to other ingredients in your store cupboard.

Mexican-style Rice

This side dish is the perfect accompaniment for chicken fajitas or flour tortillas. It is garnished with a stunning but dangerous display of flowers made from red chillies.

Serves 6

INGREDIENTS

350 g/12 oz/1¾ cups long grain rice
1 onion, chopped
2 garlic cloves, chopped
450 g/1 lb tomatoes, peeled, seeded and coarsely chopped
60 ml/4 tbsp corn or peanut oil
900 ml/1½ pints/3¾ cups chicken stock
175 g/6 oz/1½ cups peas, thawed if frozen
salt and freshly ground black pepper
fresh coriander sprigs and 4-6 red chilli flowers, to garnish

long grain rice

garlic

onion

tomatoes

corn oil

chicken stock

coriander

red chillies

peas

1 Soak the rice in a bowl of hot water for 15 minutes. Drain, rinse well under cold running water, drain again and set aside. Combine the onion, garlic and tomatoes in a food processor and process to a purée.

2 Heat the oil in a large frying pan. Add the drained rice and sauté until it becomes golden brown. Using a slotted spoon, to leave behind as much oil as possible, transfer the rice to a saucepan.

COOK'S TIP

To make chilli flowers, it is a good idea to wear rubber gloves and avoid touching your face or eyes, as the essential oils will cause a painful reaction. Slice the red chillies from tip to stem end into four or five sections. Place in a bowl of iced water until they curl back to form flowers, then drain. Wash hands or gloves thoroughly.

3 Reheat the oil remaining in the pan and cook the tomato, garlic and onion purée for 2–3 minutes. Tip it into the saucepan of rice and pour in the stock. Season to taste. Bring to the boil, reduce the heat to the lowest possible setting, cover the pan and cook for about 15–20 minutes until almost all the liquid has been absorbed.

4 Stir the peas into the rice mixture and cook, without a lid, until all the liquid has been absorbed and the rice is tender. Stir the mixture from time to time. Transfer the rice to a serving dish and garnish with the drained chilli flowers and sprigs of coriander. Warn the diners that the chilli flowers are hot and should be approached with caution.

Rice Flavoured with Saffron and Cardamom

This rice is delicately flavoured with three aromatic spices to create a superb side dish. Serve it as an accompaniment to your favourite Indian curry.

Serves 6

INGREDIENTS
450 g/1 lb/2¼ cups basmati rice
3 green cardamoms
2 cloves
5 ml/1 tsp salt
2.5 ml/½ tsp crushed saffron strands
45 ml/3 tbsp milk

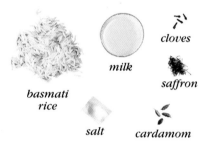

basmati rice   *milk*   *cloves*   *saffron*   *salt*   *cardamom*

1 Wash the rice thoroughly, at least twice, drain and place in a saucepan with 750 ml/1¼ pints/3 cups of water.

2 Toss the cardamoms and cloves into the saucepan along with the salt. Bring to the boil, cover, lower the heat and simmer for about 10 minutes. Meanwhile, place the saffron and milk in a small pan and warm.

COOK'S TIP

Saffron, the world's most expensive spice, is made from the stamen of the *Crocus Sativus*. Two hundred thousand flowers are harvested by hand to obtain every 450 g/1 lb saffron, which explains its high value. It is appreciated for its delicate yet distinctive flavour and striking colour, and is added to special dishes in many cuisines, savoury as well as sweet.

3 To see if the rice is fully cooked, use a slotted spoon to lift out a few grains and press the rice between your index finger and thumb. It should feel soft on the outside but still a little hard in the middle (*al dente*). Remove the pan from the heat and drain the rice through a sieve.

4 Tip the rice and whole spices back into the pan and spoon the saffron milk over the top of the rice.

5 Cover the pan with a tight-fitting lid and return to a medium heat for about 7–10 minutes. Remove the pan from the heat, leaving the lid on, and let the rice stand for a further 5 minutes before it is served.

Tomato Rice

This vibrant rice dish owes its appeal as much to the bright colours of red onion, red pepper and cherry tomatoes as it does to their luscious, distinctive flavours.

Serves 2

INGREDIENTS
115 g/4 oz/²⁄₃ cup basmati rice
30 ml/2 tbsp groundnut oil
1 small red onion, chopped
1 red pepper, seeded and chopped
225 g/8 oz cherry tomatoes, halved
2 eggs, beaten
salt and freshly ground black pepper
chopped fresh herbs, to garnish

eggs

groundnut oil

red pepper

cherry tomatoes

red onion

mixed herbs

basmati rice

COOK'S TIP

Groundnut oil is made from peanuts and has a very distinctive taste. Use it carefully at first, until you become used to the flavour. If you use groundnut oil or any peanut product, always check that none of your guests is allergic to peanuts. Use corn oil instead, if you like.

1 Wash the rice several times under cold running water. Drain well. Bring a large pan of water to the boil, add the rice and cook for 10–12 minutes.

2 Meanwhile, heat the oil in a wok until very hot. Add the onion and red pepper and stir-fry for 2–3 minutes. Add the cherry tomatoes and stir-fry for a further 2 minutes. Pour in the beaten eggs all at once.

3 Cook for 30 seconds without stirring, then stir to break up the eggs as they begin to set.

4 Drain the cooked rice thoroughly, add to the wok and toss it over the heat with the vegetable and egg mixture for 3 minutes. Season to taste. Garnish with chopped herbs.

Pigeon Peas Cook-up Rice

This Guyanese-style rice dish is made with the country's most commonly used peas. It is flavoured with creamed coconut, another popular West Indian ingredient.

Serves 4-6

INGREDIENTS
25 g/1 oz/2 tbsp butter or margarine
1 onion, chopped
1 garlic clove, crushed
25 g/1 oz/2 tbsp chopped spring
  onions
1 large carrot, diced
175 g/6 oz/about 1 cup pigeon peas
1 fresh thyme sprig or 5 ml/1 tsp
  dried thyme
1 cinnamon stick
600 ml/1 pint/2½ cups vegetable
  stock
65 g/2½ oz/4 tbsp creamed coconut
1 red chilli, chopped
450 g/1 lb/2¼ cups long grain rice
salt and freshly ground black pepper

butter

onion

cinnamon

spring onion

garlic   carrot   chilli

vegetable stock

long grain rice

creamed coconut

thyme

1 Melt the butter or margarine in a large heavy saucepan, add the chopped onion and crushed garlic and sauté over a medium heat for about 5 minutes, stirring occasionally.

COOK'S TIP

Pigeon peas are also known as gunga peas. The fresh peas can be difficult to obtain, but you will find them in specialist shops. The frozen peas are green and the canned variety are brown. Drain the salted water from canned peas and rinse before using them in this recipe.

2 Add the spring onions, carrot, pigeon peas, thyme, cinnamon, stock, creamed coconut, chilli and seasoning. Bring to the boil.

3 Reduce the heat and then stir in the rice. Cover and simmer over a low heat for about 10–15 minutes, or until all the liquid has been absorbed and the rice is tender. Stir with a fork to fluff up the rice before serving.

Rice Cakes with Cream and Mixed Mushrooms

Serve with rich meat dishes such as beef stroganoff or goulash, or as part of a vegetarian supper menu.

Serves 4

INGREDIENTS

165 g/5½ oz/¾ cup long grain rice

1 egg

15 ml/1 tbsp plain flour

60 ml/4 tbsp freshly grated Parmesan, Fontina or Pecorino cheese

50 g/2 oz/¼ cup unsalted butter, plus extra for frying rice cakes

1 small onion, chopped

175 g/6 oz/1½-2 cups assorted wild and cultivated mushrooms, trimmed and sliced

1 fresh thyme sprig

30 ml/2 tbsp Madeira or sherry

150 ml/¼ pint/⅔ cup soured cream or crème fraîche

salt and freshly ground black pepper

paprika for dusting (optional)

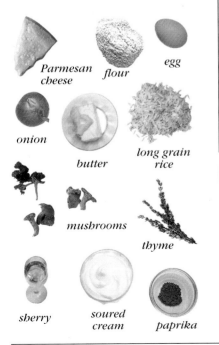

Parmesan cheese *flour* *egg*

onion *butter* *long grain rice*

mushrooms *thyme*

sherry *soured cream* *paprika*

1 Bring a saucepan of water to the boil. Add the rice and cook for about 12 minutes. Rinse, drain and cool.

2 Beat the egg, flour and cheese together with a fork, then stir in the cold cooked rice. Mix well and set aside. Melt half the butter and fry the onion until soft but not browned. Add the mushrooms and thyme and cook until the juices run. Add the Madeira or sherry. Increase the heat to reduce the juices and concentrate the flavour. Season to taste, transfer to a bowl, cover and keep hot.

3 Using a dessert spoon, shape the rice mixture into cakes. Melt a knob of butter in a frying pan and fry the rice cakes in batches for 1 minute on each side. Add more butter as needed. Keep the fried rice cakes hot.

4 When all the rice cakes are cooked, arrange on four warmed plates, top with soured cream or crème fraîche and add a spoonful of mushrooms. Dust with paprika, if using. Serve with a selection of cooked vegetables, if you like.

COOK'S TIP

Although the recipe specifies Parmesan, Fontina or Pecorino, you could use mature Cheddar cheese or even a hard goat's cheese.

Rice and Vegetable Stir-fry

If you have some left-over cooked rice and a few vegetables to spare, then you've got the basis for this quick and tasty side dish.

Serves 4

INGREDIENTS

¹/₂ cucumber
1 small red or yellow pepper
2 carrots
45 ml/3 tbsp sunflower or groundnut oil
2 spring onions, sliced
1 garlic clove, crushed
¹/₄ small green cabbage, shredded
75 g/3 oz/scant ¹/₂ cup cup long grain rice, cooked
30 ml/2 tbsp light soy sauce
15 ml/1 tbsp sesame oil
fresh parsley or coriander, chopped (optional)
115 g/4 oz/1 cup unsalted cashew nuts, almonds or peanuts
salt and freshly ground black pepper

cucumber

spring onions

carrots

garlic

pepper

green cabbage

soy sauce

long grain rice

sunflower oil

parsley

sesame oil

cashew nuts

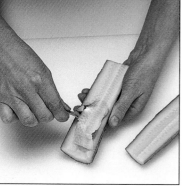

1 Halve the cucumber lengthways and scoop out the seeds with a teaspoon. Slice the flesh diagonally. Set aside.

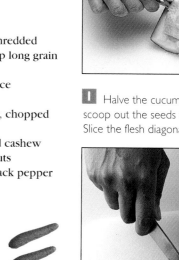

2 Cut the red or yellow pepper in half and remove the core and seeds. Slice the pepper thinly.

3 Peel the carrots and cut in thin slices. Heat the oil in a wok or large frying pan and stir-fry the sliced spring onions, garlic, carrots and pepper for 3 minutes until the vegetables are crisp but still tender.

4 Add the cabbage and cucumber and fry for another minute or two until the leaves begin to wilt. Mix in the rice, soy sauce, sesame oil and seasoning. Reheat the mixture thoroughly, stirring and tossing all the time. Add the herbs, if using, and nuts. Check the seasoning and adjust if necessary. Serve piping hot.

Sticky Rice with Tropical Fruit Topping

A popular dessert. Mangoes, with their delicate fragrance, sweet and sour flavour and velvety flesh, blend especially well with coconut sticky rice. You need to start preparing this dish the day before.

Serves 4

INGREDIENTS

115 g/4 oz/²/₃ cup glutinous (sticky)
   rice
175 ml/6 fl oz/³/₄ cup thick coconut
   milk
45 ml/3 tbsp sugar
pinch of salt
2 ripe mangoes
strips of lime rind, to decorate

*glutinous
rice*

*coconut
milk*

sugar

mangoes

lime

1 Rinse the glutinous rice thoroughly in several changes of cold water, then leave to soak overnight in a bowl of fresh, cold water. Drain and spread the rice in an even layer in a steamer lined with cheesecloth. Cover and steam for about 20 minutes or until the grains of rice are tender.

2 Meanwhile, reserve 45 ml/3 tbsp of the top of the coconut milk and combine the rest with the sugar and salt in a saucepan. Bring to the boil, stirring until the sugar dissolves, then pour into a bowl and leave to cool a little. Turn the rice into a bowl and pour over the coconut mixture. Stir, then leave for about 10–15 minutes.

3 Peel the mangoes and cut the flesh into slices. Place on top of the rice and drizzle over the reserved coconut milk. Decorate with strips of lime rind.

VARIATION

If mangoes are not available, top the sticky rice pudding with a compote, made by poaching ready-to-eat dried apricots in water to cover for about 15 minutes.

Caramel Rice

Indulge in this version of the classic sweet rice dish, which is particularly delicious when served with fresh fruit.

Serves 4

INGREDIENTS

50 g/2 oz/⅓ cup short grain pudding rice
75 ml/5 tbsp demerara sugar
pinch of salt
400 g/14 oz can evaporated milk made up to 600 ml/1 pint/2½ cups with water
knob of butter
1 small fresh pineapple
2 crisp eating apples
10 ml/2 tsp lemon juice

short grain rice

pineapple

lemon

eating apples

evaporated milk

demerara sugar

butter

1 Preheat the oven to 150°C/300°F/ Gas 2. Put the rice in a sieve and wash under running cold water. Drain well and put into a lightly greased soufflé dish. Add 30 ml/2 tbsp of the sugar and the salt to the dish. Pour on the diluted evaporated milk and stir gently. Dot the surface of the rice with butter. Bake for 2 hours in the oven, then leave to cool for about 30 minutes.

COOK'S TIP

Rice pudding is a popular dessert in many different countries, and so the possibilities for making different variations are endless. You can try sprinkling grated nutmeg on the top instead of sugar or decorate it with chopped almonds, pistachios and ground cinnamon. Rice pudding is also delicious chilled.

2 Meanwhile, peel, core and slice the pineapple and apples, then cut the pineapple into chunks. Toss the fruit in the lemon juice and set aside.

3 Preheat the grill and sprinkle the remaining sugar over the rice pudding. Grill for 5 minutes until the sugar has caramelized. Leave the rice to stand for 5 minutes to allow the caramel to harden, then serve with the fresh fruit.

Fragrant Rice Dessert with Mango Purée

Nuts, dried fruit, cardamom and rosewater make this Indian-style rice pudding a real treat.

Serves 6

INGREDIENTS
2 ripe mangoes
50 g/2 oz/scant ⅓ cup basmati rice
1.5 litres/2½ pints/6¼ cups milk
50 g/2 oz/¼ cup demerara sugar
50 g/2 oz/⅓ cup sultanas
5 ml/1 tsp rosewater
5 green cardamoms
45 ml/3 tbsp orange juice
45 ml/3 tbsp flaked almonds, toasted
45 ml/3 tbsp pistachio nuts, chopped

mangoes

sultanas

basmati rice

orange juice

milk

demerara sugar

cardamom

flaked almonds

pistachio nuts

1 Using a sharp knife, peel, slice and stone the mangoes.

2 Preheat the oven to 150°C/300°F/Gas 2. Put the basmati rice in an ovenproof dish. Bring the milk to the boil in a saucepan, then pour it over the rice. Bake uncovered for 2 hours until the rice has become soft and mushy.

3 Remove the dish from the oven and stir in the demerara sugar and sultanas, with half the rosewater. Crush the cardamom pods, extract the seeds and stir them into the rice mixture. Allow to cool.

4 Place the mango flesh in a blender or food processor. Add the orange juice and remaining rosewater. Blend until smooth. Divide the mango purée among six individual glass serving dishes. Spoon the rice pudding mixture evenly over the top. Leave to chill thoroughly in the fridge. When ready to serve, scatter the toasted almonds and chopped pistachio nuts over the top of each pudding.

VARIATION
Make this nutritious dessert an even healthier option by decorating with slices of fruit instead of nuts.

Mexican Rice Pudding

Here is another delicious version of the classic rice dessert. This Mexican recipe – *Arroz con Leche* – is light and attractive and combines many tantalizing flavours. It is surprisingly easy to make.

Serves 4

INGREDIENTS

75 g/3 oz/½ cup raisins
90 g/3½ oz/½ cup short grain rice
2.5 cm/1 in strip of pared lime or lemon rind
475 ml/16 fl oz/2 cups milk
225 g/8 oz/1 cup granulated sugar
1.5 ml/¼ tsp salt
2.5 cm/1 in piece of cinnamon stick
2 egg yolks, well beaten
15 g/½ oz/1 tbsp unsalted butter, cubed
toasted flaked almonds to decorate
segments of fresh peeled oranges, to serve

raisins

short grain rice

milk

cinnamon

lime

eggs

oranges

sugar

butter

flaked almonds

1 Soak the raisins in warm water to cover until plump. Place the rice in a saucepan with 250 ml/8 fl oz/1 cup water and the citrus rind. Bring slowly to the boil, then cover and simmer for 20 minutes until the water is absorbed.

2 Remove the rind from the rice and discard it. Add the milk, sugar, salt and cinnamon and cook, stirring, over a very low heat until all the milk has been absorbed. Do not cover the pan.

3 Discard the cinnamon stick. Beat in the egg yolks. Drain the raisins well and stir them into the rice. Add the cubed butter and stir until it has melted and the pudding is rich and creamy. Cook the pudding for a few minutes longer.

4 Scrape the rice into a dish and cool. Decorate with the almonds and serve with the orange segments.

Rice Pudding with Mixed Berry Sauce

An irresistible combination of creamy rice with refreshing summer fruits that gives a new meaning to the phrase "comfort food".

Serves 6

INGREDIENTS
400 g/14 oz/2 cups short grain rice
300 ml/½ pint/1¼ cups milk
pinch of salt
115 g/4 oz/⅔ cup soft light brown
    sugar
5 ml/1 tsp vanilla essence
2 eggs, beaten
grated rind of 1 lemon
5 ml/1 tsp fresh lemon juice
25 g/1 oz/2 tbsp butter or margarine
strawberry leaves, to decorate
    (optional)

FOR THE SAUCE
175 g/6 oz/1¼ cups strawberries,
    hulled and quartered
225 g/8 oz/1½ cups raspberries
115 g/4 oz/½ cup granulated sugar
grated rind of 1 lemon

short grain rice *vanilla essence* *eggs* *lemon*

milk *light brown sugar* *butter*

raspberries *strawberries* *sugar*

1 Preheat the oven to 160°C/325°F/ Gas 3. Grease a 1 litre/1¾ pint/4 cup baking dish. Bring a saucepan of water to the boil. Add the rice and boil for 5 minutes. Drain. Transfer the rice to the prepared baking dish.

2 In a bowl, combine the milk, salt, brown sugar, vanilla, eggs, and lemon rind and juice. Pour this mixture over the rice and stir well. Dot the surface of the rice mixture with the butter or margarine. Bake for about 50 minutes, until the rice is cooked and creamy.

3 Meanwhile, make the sauce. Mix the berries and granulated sugar in a small saucepan. Stir over a low heat until the sugar has dissolved completely and the fruit is becoming pulpy. Transfer to a bowl and stir in the lemon rind. Chill the sauce until required.

4 Remove the rice pudding from the oven. Allow to cool completely, and serve with the berry sauce. Decorate with strawberry leaves, if you like.

Thai-style Dessert

Black glutinous rice, also known as black sticky rice, makes a tasty pudding. It tastes nutty, rather like wild rice.

Serves 4-6

INGREDIENTS
175 g/6 oz/scant 1 cup black
    glutinous (sticky) rice
30 ml/2 tbsp soft light brown sugar
475 ml/16 fl oz/2 cups coconut milk
3 eggs
30 ml/2 tbsp granulated sugar

soft light
brown sugar

coconut
milk

eggs

black glutinous
rice

granulated
sugar

1 Combine the glutinous rice, brown sugar, half the coconut milk and 250 ml/ 8 fl oz/1 cup of water in a saucepan. Bring to the boil, then simmer for about 15–20 minutes or until the rice has absorbed most of the liquid, stirring from time to time. Preheat the oven to 150°C/300°F/Gas 2.

2 Transfer the rice into one large ovenproof dish or divide it among individual ramekins. Mix the eggs, remaining coconut milk and granulated sugar in a bowl. Strain and pour the mixture evenly over the rice mixture.

3 Place the dish or ramekins in a baking tin. Pour in enough boiling water to come halfway up the sides of the dishes. Cover with foil and bake in the oven for about 35 minutes to 1 hour or until the custard is set. Serve warm or cold, whichever you prefer.

VARIATION
Black glutinous rice is popular in South-east Asia for sweet dishes. Its character contributes to the delicious flavour of this dessert. Use white glutinous rice if the black grain is difficult to find.

COOK'S TIP
A pan of water in which dishes of delicate food are cooked, is known as a *bain marie*.

INDEX